Age of Pirates

The Rise and Fall of the Caribbean Sea Wolves

Arthur Weiss

Copyright ©2024 All rights reserved

The content contained within this book may not be reproduced, duplicated or transmitted without direct written permission from the author or the publisher.

Under no circumstances will any blame or legal responsibility be held against the publisher, or author, for any damages, reparation, or monetary loss due to the information contained within this book, either directly or indirectly.

Legal Notice: This book is copyright protected. This book is only for personal use. You cannot amend, distribute, sell, use, quote or paraphrase any part, or the content within this book, without the consent of the author or publisher.

Disclaimer Notice: Please note the information contained within this document is for educational and entertainment purposes only. All effort has been executed to present accurate, up to date, and reliable, complete information. Readers acknowledge that the author is not engaging in the rendering of legal, financial, medical or professional advice.

By reading this document, the reader agrees that under no circumstances is the author responsible for any losses, direct or indirect, which are incurred as a result of the use of the information contained within this document, including, but not limited to, — errors, omissions, or inaccuracies.

Table of Contents

Intro: The Allure of the Caribbean _____ 5

Chapter 1: The Dawn of the Sea Wolves _____ 11

Chapter 2: The Golden Age Begins _____ 28

Chapter 3: Pirate Tactics and Ships _____ 41

Chapter 4: Life Aboard the Ship _____ 52

Chapter 5: The Legends of the Sea _____ 63

Chapter 6: Pirate Myths and Mysteries _____ 87

Chapter 7: The Consequences of Piracy _____ 100

Chapter 8: The Decline of the Golden Age _____ 107

Afterword _____ 124

Intro: The Allure of the Caribbean

The Caribbean Sea, with its turquoise waters and lush, tropical islands, has long been romanticized as a paradise. Yet, for centuries, it was a theater of fierce competition, lawlessness, and economic ambition. The allure of the Caribbean during the Age of Piracy was deeply rooted in its geopolitical significance, strategic positioning, and the wealth it funneled from the New World to the Old. To understand why this region became a hotspot for piracy, we must examine the unique interplay of geography, colonial rivalries, and the immense flow of treasure through its waters.

Gateway Between the Old and New Worlds

The Caribbean's geographic location made it an essential crossroads for the colonial empires of Spain, England, France, and the Netherlands. Positioned between the Americas, Europe, and Africa, the region became a hub for transatlantic trade. Ships laden with gold, silver, sugar, tobacco, and other valuable commodities regularly traversed its waters, bound for European markets.

The islands themselves served as crucial waypoints for resupplying and repairing ships during long ocean voyages. Natural harbors, hidden coves, and uncharted inlets provided ideal hiding spots, not just for legitimate naval vessels but for pirates as well. These features made the

Caribbean an irresistible hunting ground for those willing to seize their fortune by force.

The Wealth of the Spanish Main

The Spanish Main, a term used to describe Spain's colonial mainland territories in the Americas, was a primary source of the wealth that fueled piracy. Spain's vast empire in the New World included resource-rich colonies such as Mexico and Peru, which produced staggering quantities of gold and silver. The Spanish treasure fleets, meticulously organized convoys of galleons, transported these riches from the Americas to Spain via Caribbean ports like Havana and Cartagena.

These fleets were irresistible targets for pirates. A single captured galleon could yield a lifetime's worth of treasure. The predictable routes and timing of the treasure fleets made them vulnerable, despite their heavily armed escorts. For pirates, the potential reward far outweighed the risk.

Colonial Rivalries and Opportunism

The Age of Piracy coincided with an era of intense rivalry among European powers. Spain, the dominant colonial force in the early years, faced growing competition from England, France, and the Netherlands. These nations, eager to undermine Spain's monopoly on New World wealth, often turned a blind eye to—or even encouraged—piracy against Spanish ships and settlements.

Privateering, a legal form of piracy sanctioned by governments, blurred the lines between legitimate naval warfare and outright theft. Privateers like Sir Francis

Drake, operating under letters of marque, targeted Spanish vessels with the blessing of the English Crown. Many of these privateers turned to full-fledged piracy when peace treaties revoked their commissions, creating a pool of seasoned sailors eager to plunder.

The Promise of Freedom

For many, the Caribbean represented more than just economic opportunity; it was a place where the rigid hierarchies of European society could be subverted. The promise of quick riches drew not only seasoned sailors but also outcasts, adventurers, and escaped slaves seeking a life of relative freedom. The multicultural crews aboard pirate ships reflected the diverse populations of the Caribbean colonies.

The islands themselves became pirate havens. Nassau in the Bahamas, Port Royal in Jamaica, and Tortuga off the coast of Hispaniola were infamous for their lawlessness and open acceptance of piracy. These locations provided safe harbors where pirates could repair ships, trade stolen goods, and enjoy the spoils of their conquests.

The Caribbean's role as a hotspot for piracy was a natural outcome of its strategic importance and the intense competition among colonial empires. The combination of immense wealth, navigable seas, and fragmented political control created a perfect storm for piracy to thrive. As empires jockeyed for dominance, pirates exploited the chaos, turning the Caribbean into a proving ground for their audacious exploits.

Exploration and Colonization

The Age of Exploration, which began in the late fifteenth century, marked the beginning of unprecedented global maritime expansion. European powers, driven by the pursuit of wealth, territorial expansion, and religious missionizing, launched voyages that reshaped the known world. While these explorations laid the groundwork for vast colonial empires, they also inadvertently created the perfect conditions for piracy to flourish, particularly in the Caribbean. This region, with its strategic location and rich resources, became a crucible of opportunity and conflict that attracted not only settlers and traders but also outlaws and opportunists.

Spain led the charge into the New World following Christopher Columbus's voyages. The discovery of vast gold and silver deposits in territories such as Mexico and Peru transformed the Spanish empire into the wealthiest power in Europe. This wealth flowed back to Spain along a carefully managed maritime network, with the Caribbean serving as a crucial staging area for the transport of treasures. Ports such as Havana, Santo Domingo, and Cartagena de Indias became critical hubs for processing and shipping resources extracted from the Americas. The seas surrounding these colonies became highways for the Spanish treasure fleets, which carried immense fortunes across the Atlantic.

However, Spain's monopoly on New World wealth was a tempting prize for its rivals. England, France, and the Netherlands, excluded from the spoils of Spanish conquests by treaties like the Treaty of Tordesillas, sought alternative ways to profit from the Americas. Initially, these powers focused on establishing colonies of their own in the Caribbean and along the Atlantic coast of North America. Yet, as their settlements struggled to take root, they also turned to more direct methods of wealth acquisition: raiding Spanish ships and settlements. This early competition sowed the seeds of piracy, as the weak colonial presence of non-Spanish powers in the region provided limited enforcement against maritime raiding.

The expansion of maritime trade routes during this period further set the stage for piracy. The Americas became central to the emerging global economy, linking Europe, Africa, and the New World in a vast exchange of goods and labor. Ships carried gold, silver, sugar, tobacco, and other lucrative commodities back to European markets. They returned laden with European goods and, tragically, human cargo from Africa, fueling the transatlantic slave trade. This constant flow of high-value goods created a wealth of opportunity for those willing to take it by force. Merchant ships, often poorly armed and crewed, made for easy prey, and the predictable routes of treasure fleets and cargo vessels offered pirates a tactical advantage.

Adding to the volatility was the practice of privateering. During periods of war, European governments issued letters of marque to private shipowners, authorizing them to attack and plunder enemy vessels. While privateering was a legal form of warfare, it blurred the lines between legitimate naval combat and piracy. Many privateers, lured by the profits of raiding, continued their activities even after their commissions were revoked during peacetime. The result was a population of skilled, well-armed sailors who operated outside the bounds of law. These privateers-turned-pirates found in the Caribbean a theater where weak colonial enforcement and abundant targets allowed them to thrive.

The fragmentation of colonial authority in the Caribbean was another critical factor. The colonies were often poorly governed, with vast distances separating them from European centers of power. Many local governors turned a blind eye to piracy, particularly when it targeted rival nations. In some cases, they actively collaborated with pirates, providing them with safe harbors in exchange for a share of their loot or goods at cut-rate prices. Islands like Tortuga and Port Royal became infamous pirate enclaves, offering protection and trade networks that enabled raiders to sustain their operations.

As European empires expanded into the Americas, they brought with them not only the promise of wealth but also a culture of competition and conflict that undermined their ability to control the region. The lure of untold riches, the vulnerability of maritime trade, and the fractured authority of colonial administrations combined to create an environment in which piracy could flourish. The Caribbean, at the intersection of these forces, became the proving ground for the audacious sea wolves of the Golden Age of Piracy. The very ambitions that drove European exploration and colonization thus unwittingly fueled the rise of piracy, ensuring that the region's history would be as much about rebellion and lawlessness as it was about imperial conquest and trade.

Chapter 1: The Dawn of the Sea Wolves

Origins of Piracy

Piracy, as a practice of maritime robbery and plunder, has existed as long as humans have traversed the seas. Long before the Golden Age of Piracy in the Caribbean, piracy had established itself as a persistent menace in ancient and medieval history. The earliest records of piracy highlight its deep connection to trade routes, seafaring technology, and the vulnerabilities of maritime commerce. From the predatory Sea Peoples of the Bronze Age to the Viking marauders of medieval Europe, piracy has been a recurring phenomenon, shaped by the geography and political dynamics of its time.

In the ancient world, piracy emerged alongside the development of early maritime trade. The Mediterranean Sea, with its interconnected networks of ports and trade routes, was particularly vulnerable to pirate activity. The Sea Peoples, a mysterious coalition of raiders from the 13th century BCE, are among the earliest known pirates. These marauders, whose origins remain a topic of scholarly debate, targeted coastal cities and merchant vessels across the eastern Mediterranean. Their attacks disrupted trade and contributed to the decline of powerful civilizations, including the Hittite Empire and the Egyptian New Kingdom.

Piracy persisted throughout the classical era, becoming a chronic problem for ancient Greek city-states and later for the Roman Republic. The Aegean Sea, with its numerous islands and hidden coves, provided ideal hiding places for pirates who preyed on merchant ships carrying goods such as grain, wine, and olive oil. In Greek mythology, piracy was a common theme, reflecting its prevalence in the real world. Homer's *Odyssey* contains references to raiding and looting, illustrating how ingrained these activities were in the cultural fabric of the time.

By the 1st century BCE, piracy in the Mediterranean reached a crisis point. The Cilician pirates, based in the rugged coastal regions of modern-day Turkey, became infamous for their audacity and organization. They targeted not only cargo ships but also wealthy travelers, including Roman citizens, whom they captured and ransomed. Their activities disrupted Rome's grain supply from Egypt, threatening the stability of the empire. In response, the Roman general Pompey the Great launched a massive naval campaign to eradicate piracy in 67 BCE. Within three months, he subdued the Cilician pirates, securing the Mediterranean and cementing Rome's dominance over its trade routes.

In medieval Europe, piracy adapted to the changing political and economic landscape. The decline of centralized authority following the fall of the Roman Empire created opportunities for local warlords and seafaring raiders to exploit coastal settlements and maritime trade. The Viking Age, which began in the late 8th century, marked one of the most infamous periods of piracy in European history. Norse raiders from Scandinavia launched devastating attacks on monasteries, towns, and merchant vessels across the British Isles, the Frankish Empire, and beyond. Their longships, designed for speed and shallow-water navigation, allowed them to strike swiftly and retreat before organized resistance could form.

While Vikings are often romanticized as explorers and settlers, their raids were fundamentally acts of piracy. They sought treasure, livestock, and slaves, which they either used to bolster their own societies or traded for goods. The fear of Viking raids profoundly shaped the political and social structures of medieval Europe, prompting the construction of fortified towns and the development of early naval defenses.

Piracy was not confined to Europe and the Mediterranean. In Asia, maritime raiding was a common practice among coastal communities and seafaring empires. During the Tang and Song dynasties in China, pirates operating in the South China Sea targeted trade routes connecting China to Southeast Asia and the Indian Ocean. These pirates disrupted the lucrative spice trade, compelling governments to invest in naval fleets and coastal fortifications.

Similarly, in the Indian Ocean, piracy flourished along the trade routes linking East Africa, the Arabian Peninsula, India, and Southeast Asia. The Malacca Strait, a vital chokepoint for maritime trade, became a hotspot for pirate activity. These pirates, often local fishermen or traders driven by economic necessity, targeted merchant ships carrying spices, textiles, and precious metals.

Throughout history, piracy has thrived wherever trade routes intersected with weak governance and economic inequality. Pirates exploited the vulnerabilities of maritime commerce, seizing wealth and disrupting economies. While their methods and motivations varied across cultures and eras, pirates consistently capitalized on the opportunities created by the sea—a vast, ungoverned space where the risks were high, but the potential rewards were even higher.

The origins of piracy reveal a pattern that would repeat itself in later centuries, including during the Golden Age of Piracy in the Caribbean. The combination of lucrative trade, insufficient naval enforcement, and the allure of wealth proved to be a powerful draw for individuals willing to risk their lives for a chance at fortune.

Spanish Conquests and the Treasure Fleets

The Spanish conquests of the Americas in the late 15th and early 16th centuries reshaped the geopolitical and economic landscape of the Western Hemisphere. With the discovery of vast mineral wealth in territories like Mexico and Peru, Spain rapidly established itself as the dominant colonial power of the era. The riches extracted from the New World—primarily gold and silver—became the foundation of Spain's imperial economy and fueled its ambitions in Europe and beyond. At the heart of this economic engine were the Spanish treasure fleets, an extraordinary maritime system designed to transport wealth across the Atlantic. The rise of this system transformed the Caribbean into a vital conduit for global trade and, simultaneously, a tempting hunting ground for pirates and privateers.

The story of the treasure fleets begins with the Spanish conquest of the Aztec and Inca empires. In the early 16th century, Hernán Cortés defeated the Aztecs in present-day Mexico, while Francisco Pizarro dismantled the Inca Empire in Peru. These conquests opened access to staggering quantities of gold, silver, and other resources. The Spanish quickly established mining operations, with Peru's Potosí silver mines becoming one of the most significant sources of wealth in the world. These mines alone produced hundreds of tons of silver annually, enriching the Spanish Crown and fueling the global economy.

The Caribbean played a central role in the extraction and transportation of this wealth. Spanish colonies in the region, such as Havana, Santo Domingo, and Cartagena de Indias, served as strategic hubs where treasure was gathered, stored, and shipped. The region's ports became essential waypoints for Spanish ships traveling to and from the Americas. Havana, in particular, emerged as a key staging ground for the treasure fleets, offering both a secure harbor and a well-defended position to protect Spain's maritime interests.

The treasure fleets, known as the *flota system*, were a marvel of logistical organization. To safeguard the immense wealth being transported, Spain implemented a convoy system that grouped merchant ships under the protection of armed galleons. These fleets sailed twice a year, with one convoy departing from Veracruz, Mexico, and another from Cartagena, collecting silver, gold, gemstones, and other valuables from across the Spanish colonies. The ships then rendezvoused in Havana before making the perilous journey across the Atlantic to Seville, Spain.

While this system was highly effective at consolidating and protecting wealth, it was not without vulnerabilities. The treasure fleets followed predictable routes and schedules, making them prime targets for pirates and privateers. These convoys carried such extraordinary riches that even a single successful attack could yield a fortune. The prospect of capturing a treasure fleet inspired many daring raids, including those led by infamous figures like Sir Francis Drake and Henry Morgan.

The immense flow of wealth through the Caribbean had profound consequences. For Spain, the influx of precious metals strengthened its economy and allowed it to finance military campaigns and territorial expansion in Europe. However, this wealth also had destabilizing effects, including rampant inflation and overreliance on New World resources. The vast treasures extracted from the Americas fueled conflicts with rival European powers, who sought to undermine Spain's dominance through war and piracy.

For the Caribbean itself, the treasure fleets transformed the region into a theater of competition and conflict. The promise of immense wealth attracted not only settlers and traders but also privateers and pirates eager to seize their share. Coastal cities and islands became frequent targets of raids, with fortifications springing up across the region to defend against attacks. The Spanish colonies became heavily militarized, with fortresses like Castillo de San Marcos in St. Augustine and the Castillo de San Felipe de Barajas in Cartagena standing as testaments to Spain's efforts to protect its wealth.

The treasure fleets also played a significant role in shaping global trade. The silver transported from the Americas found its way into European markets, where it was used to finance trade with Asia. Chinese merchants, in particular, valued silver as a medium of exchange, creating a vast economic network that linked the Americas, Europe, and Asia. The treasure fleets were not merely a Spanish enterprise; they were a cornerstone of the emerging global economy, connecting distant regions through the flow of wealth.

Despite their successes, the treasure fleets eventually became emblematic of Spain's declining fortunes. By the late 17th century, Spain faced growing challenges from rival powers and internal economic difficulties. The decline of the treasure fleets mirrored the broader weakening of Spanish dominance in the Americas. Yet their legacy endures as a symbol of both the extraordinary wealth extracted from the New World and the intense competition that defined the age of exploration and colonization.

The rise of the treasure fleets marked a turning point in Caribbean history, transforming the region into a critical nexus of global trade and imperial ambition. Their wealth enriched empires, inspired daring acts of piracy, and shaped the economic and political landscapes of the early modern world.

The Impact of Privateering

Privateering was a sanctioned form of maritime raiding that existed in the gray area between warfare and piracy. It allowed governments to authorize private shipowners to attack and plunder enemy vessels during times of war, offering a way to weaken rivals while enriching individuals and supporting naval efforts without the expense of maintaining large standing fleets. These sanctioned raiders, known as privateers, carried letters of marque—official documents issued by their governments granting them the legal right to target enemy ships. However, the practice of privateering not only blurred the lines between legitimate naval activity and piracy but also had profound economic, political, and cultural consequences, particularly in the Caribbean during the Age of Exploration and Colonization.

Privateering emerged as a practical solution for nations with limited naval resources. In the 16th and 17th centuries, European powers, particularly England, France, and the Netherlands, relied heavily on privateers to challenge Spain's dominance in the Americas. Spain's treasure fleets, laden with gold, silver, and other valuable commodities, became irresistible targets for rival powers eager to disrupt Spanish hegemony and claim a share of the New World's wealth. By issuing letters of marque to private shipowners, these governments effectively outsourced naval warfare, enabling them to strike at Spanish interests without deploying their official navies.

For privateers, the appeal was obvious. The letters of marque granted them legal immunity from prosecution for acts that would otherwise be considered piracy. These documents provided a veneer of legitimacy, transforming plundering into an act of patriotic service. In return, privateers were required to share a portion of their spoils with their sponsoring government, creating a mutually beneficial arrangement. The profits from privateering could be substantial, offering the promise of immense wealth to those willing to risk the dangers of maritime combat.

However, the distinction between privateering and piracy was often tenuous at best. The effectiveness of privateering depended on its inherently opportunistic and predatory nature, which made it difficult to regulate. Many privateers operated with little oversight, targeting not only enemy ships but also neutral and even allied vessels under the pretext of confusion or self-defense. Some privateers, emboldened by their successes and motivated by greed, continued raiding after the wars ended or expanded their activities to include outright piracy. These rogue privateers blurred the line between lawful and unlawful raiding, becoming indistinguishable from the pirates they were ostensibly different from.

The Caribbean became a particularly fertile ground for privateering, with its busy trade routes, valuable cargoes, and contested waters. During conflicts such as the Anglo-Spanish War (1585–1604) and the War of the Spanish Succession (1701–1714), privateers played a crucial role in disrupting enemy commerce. Figures like Sir Francis Drake, who began his career as a privateer under Queen

Elizabeth I, became celebrated heroes in their home countries despite their actions being regarded as criminal by their enemies. Drake's raids on Spanish ports and treasure fleets, for example, severely disrupted Spain's flow of wealth from the Americas and emboldened England's challenge to Spanish dominance.

Yet the practice of privateering also had destabilizing effects. The influx of wealth generated by privateering often undermined local economies, fostering corruption and lawlessness. Port cities like Port Royal in Jamaica and Tortuga in Hispaniola became notorious havens for privateers and pirates alike, their economies thriving on stolen goods. These ports blurred the line further by providing safe harbors and markets for contraband, making it nearly impossible to distinguish between legitimate privateering enterprises and illegal piracy.

The eventual decline of privateering highlighted its problematic legacy. By the 18th century, as European powers sought to establish more stable and controlled colonial economies, privateering became increasingly viewed as a liability. The Peace of Utrecht in 1713, which ended the War of the Spanish Succession, marked a turning point. With the cessation of hostilities, many privateers found themselves out of work, their letters of marque rendered void. Some returned to civilian life, but many others turned to piracy, unwilling to abandon the lucrative, albeit illegal, practices they had mastered during the war. The resulting surge in piracy in the early 18th century, often referred to as the Golden Age of Piracy, was fueled in part by these disillusioned former privateers.

Privateering also left a lasting cultural imprint, shaping the romanticized image of pirates as adventurous and daring figures. While privateers operated under legal authority, their exploits were often indistinguishable from those of pirates in the public imagination. The blurred lines between privateering and piracy helped to create a narrative in which the two became intertwined, reinforcing the notion of the swashbuckling rogue hero.

Ultimately, privateering was a double-edged sword. While it provided European powers with a cost-effective means of waging economic warfare, it also contributed to the chaos and instability of maritime trade. The practice exposed the inherent contradictions of a system that sought to regulate lawlessness while relying on the very behaviors it aimed to control. By legitimizing and rewarding the act of plundering, privateering laid the groundwork for the lawlessness that would characterize the high seas for centuries to come.

Early Pirates: François Le Clerc and John Hawkins

François Le Clerc, better known by his fearsome moniker "Jambe de Bois," or "Peg Leg," was one of the most notorious and ambitious pirates of the 16th century. Born in France, likely in the early 1500s, Le Clerc rose to prominence as a privateer and pirate during a period of fierce geopolitical rivalry between European powers. His career was marked by audacious raids on Spanish territories, a relentless quest for wealth, and a reputation for ruthlessness that made him a symbol of early piracy.

Le Clerc's maritime career began in the service of the French Crown during the reign of King Francis I. France, eager to challenge Spain's dominance in the New World, issued letters of marque to privateers like Le Clerc, granting them legal authority to attack Spanish ships and settlements. These privateers were seen as valuable tools in undermining Spain's colonial empire, which had become a source of immense wealth thanks to the extraction of gold and silver from the Americas.

Le Clerc quickly distinguished himself through his tactical brilliance and daring. His nickname, "Jambe de Bois," derived from the wooden prosthetic leg he wore after losing a limb in battle. This physical impairment did little to hinder his activities and may have even added to his fearsome persona. As a leader, he commanded loyalty and respect from his crew, a mix of seasoned sailors, adventurers, and outlaws drawn by the promise of plunder.

One of Le Clerc's most infamous exploits occurred in 1553, when he led a fleet of privateers in a devastating attack on Santiago, the capital of Hispaniola (modern-day Dominican Republic). Santiago was a vital hub for Spanish colonial operations, and its wealth made it a prime target. Le Clerc's fleet overwhelmed the city's defenses, sacking and burning much of it while looting valuable goods. This raid not only enriched Le Clerc and his crew but also exposed the vulnerabilities of Spain's colonial infrastructure.

The success of the Santiago raid solidified Le Clerc's reputation as a master of maritime warfare. That same year, he turned his attention to the Azores, a strategically important archipelago that served as a waypoint for Spanish treasure ships returning from the Americas. Le Clerc's attacks on Spanish shipping lanes in the region disrupted the flow of wealth that underpinned Spain's empire. By targeting both coastal settlements and merchant vessels, he demonstrated a deep understanding of the interconnected trade networks that sustained Spanish colonial dominance.

Le Clerc's raids were not driven solely by loyalty to France. Like many privateers, his actions were as much about personal enrichment as they were about serving his nation. While he operated under the guise of legality provided by letters of marque, his methods often mirrored those of outright piracy. For the Spanish, there was little distinction between privateers like Le Clerc and the pirates who terrorized their ships and settlements. His name became synonymous with destruction and terror along Spain's Atlantic and Caribbean routes.

Despite his successes, Le Clerc's career was shaped by the inherent risks and uncertainties of piracy. The shifting political landscape of the mid-16th century often left privateers in precarious positions. Peace treaties between rival nations could invalidate letters of marque, leaving privateers vulnerable to prosecution as pirates. Additionally, the rise of more robust naval defenses in Spanish territories made raids increasingly dangerous.

By the late 1550s, Le Clerc's activities began to wane. Accounts of his later life are sparse, and it is unclear whether he retired or met his end in battle. Some historians suggest that he may have returned to France to live out his remaining years, while others speculate that he continued raiding until his death. Regardless of his fate, Le Clerc's impact on the history of piracy is undeniable.

François Le Clerc was a figure of both admiration and fear. For the French, he was a patriot who struck at the heart of their greatest rival. For the Spanish, he was a scourge whose name evoked images of burning cities and plundered ships.

John Hawkins

John Hawkins was a pivotal figure in the history of English seafaring, a man whose career straddled the line between explorer, trader, privateer, and statesman. Born in 1532 in Plymouth, England, Hawkins rose to prominence during the reign of Queen Elizabeth I, a period of growing English maritime ambition. Known for his innovations in ship design, his role in the transatlantic slave trade, and his audacious raids on Spanish interests.

Hawkins was born into a family deeply rooted in maritime tradition. His father, William Hawkins, was a prominent sea captain and one of the first Englishmen to trade with the Portuguese colonies in Africa and Brazil. From a young age, John Hawkins was immersed in the world of navigation and trade, learning the skills that would define his career. As England sought to expand its influence on the seas, Hawkins became one of the leading figures in its maritime efforts.

One of the most controversial aspects of Hawkins's career was his involvement in the transatlantic slave trade. In the 1560s, Hawkins undertook a series of voyages to West

Africa, where he acquired enslaved people—through both trade and violent raids—and transported them across the Atlantic to the Spanish colonies in the Americas. His first slaving voyage, in 1562, was backed by influential financiers, including members of the English nobility. Hawkins sold the enslaved Africans in Spanish settlements such as Santo Domingo, using the profits to purchase valuable commodities like sugar and pearls. Despite the illegality of trading with Spanish colonies—due to Spain's mercantile laws restricting commerce to Spanish merchants—Hawkins's voyages were initially highly profitable.

Hawkins's success caught the attention of Queen Elizabeth I, who supported his second voyage in 1564 by lending him a ship, the Jesus of Lübeck. This royal endorsement marked Hawkins as a favorite of the Crown and provided him with the resources to expand his operations. However, his activities also drew the ire of Spain, whose colonial monopoly he repeatedly violated. The Spanish viewed Hawkins as a threat to their empire and an example of England's growing willingness to challenge Spanish dominance in the Americas.

Hawkins's third voyage in 1567 ended disastrously and marked a turning point in his career. Partnering with his young cousin Francis Drake, Hawkins set out with a fleet of six ships to trade enslaved Africans in the Spanish colonies. After some initial successes, the fleet was ambushed by Spanish forces at the port of San Juan de Ulúa in present-day Mexico. The Spanish, determined to defend their territories, attacked Hawkins's fleet, resulting in heavy losses. Only two ships, including Hawkins's flagship

Minion, escaped, and many of his men were killed or captured. Hawkins returned to England with his reputation tarnished but his resolve to oppose Spain strengthened.

Following this setback, Hawkins pivoted toward privateering, aligning himself more closely with England's broader strategy of undermining Spanish power. As a privateer, he raided Spanish ships and settlements, enriching himself and contributing to England's naval expansion. Hawkins's efforts laid the groundwork for England's emergence as a maritime power, and his experience in shipbuilding proved invaluable. He introduced design improvements that made English ships faster, more maneuverable, and better suited for combat. These innovations would later prove crucial during the conflict with the Spanish Armada.

Hawkins's career culminated in his role as one of the principal commanders of the English fleet during the Spanish Armada's attempted invasion of England in 1588. Serving alongside luminaries such as Sir Francis Drake and Lord Charles Howard, Hawkins was instrumental in the English victory. His naval tactics, combined with the superior maneuverability of the English ships, allowed the fleet to outmatch the larger and more heavily armed Spanish galleons. The defeat of the Armada marked a turning point in European history, signaling the decline of Spain's naval dominance and the rise of England as a global maritime power.

In the later years of his life, Hawkins took on administrative roles, including serving as Treasurer of the Royal Navy. In this capacity, he worked to modernize and expand the fleet, ensuring that England remained prepared for future conflicts. Despite his accomplishments, Hawkins's legacy is deeply intertwined with the darker aspects of his career, particularly his role in the slave trade. While he was celebrated in his time as a national hero and pioneer, his involvement in the exploitation and suffering of enslaved Africans casts a long shadow over his achievements.

John Hawkins died in 1595 during a failed expedition to the West Indies, an ambitious venture intended to raid Spanish territories in partnership with Francis Drake.

Chapter 2: The Golden Age Begins

The Buccaneers of Hispaniola

The buccaneers of Hispaniola emerged in the 17th century as a unique and influential group of seafarers who embodied the volatile mix of opportunity, desperation, and ambition that characterized the Caribbean. Originally hunters and subsistence farmers living on the fringes of European colonial society, these men transitioned into piracy and privateering, becoming some of the most notorious figures in the region's turbulent history.

Hispaniola, the first island in the Americas to be colonized by Europeans, was initially a stronghold of Spanish influence. However, by the early 17th century, Spain had shifted its focus to more lucrative territories in mainland America, leaving much of Hispaniola underdeveloped and sparsely populated. This neglect created a vacuum that drew marginalized groups, including runaway slaves, indigenous people, and European settlers seeking refuge from the rigid hierarchies of colonial life. Among them were French and English settlers who established small communities on the island and its nearby satellite, Tortuga.

These settlers earned their livelihood primarily as hunters. They specialized in hunting the wild cattle and pigs that roamed freely on Hispaniola, descendants of animals introduced by the Spanish. The meat they produced, often smoked or cured, became known as "boucan," a term derived from the indigenous Taíno word for a type of smoking rack. From this practice, the term "buccaneer" emerged, originally referring to these hunters and later expanding to describe their piratical successors.

The transition from hunting to piracy was gradual but inevitable. The buccaneers' isolated existence, combined with their familiarity with firearms and small-scale organization, made them well-suited to the dangerous and opportunistic world of maritime raiding. Their initial ventures into piracy were often driven by necessity. As Spanish authorities sought to eliminate their settlements and control the trade in meat and hides, the buccaneers turned to raiding Spanish ships and settlements in retaliation. Over time, these acts of reprisal evolved into a more systematic and lucrative form of piracy.

The buccaneers' rise coincided with the broader geopolitical struggles of the Caribbean. Spain's dominance in the region was increasingly challenged by rival European powers, including England, France, and the Netherlands. These nations frequently relied on privateers to weaken Spanish control, and the buccaneers, with their combat skills and knowledge of the region, became valuable allies. Buccaneer leaders like Jean-David Nau, better known as François l'Olonnais, and Henry Morgan gained notoriety for their audacious attacks on Spanish territories, often operating with the tacit or explicit support of European governments.

Tortuga, a small island off the northern coast of Hispaniola, became a key base for the buccaneers. Initially settled by a mix of French and English colonists, Tortuga developed into a lawless haven for pirates, privateers, and adventurers. Its strategic location, close to Spanish shipping routes, made it an ideal staging ground for raids. The island's rugged terrain provided natural defenses, while its lack of strong governance allowed the buccaneers to operate with relative impunity.

Life as a buccaneer was harsh and unpredictable. Although some raids yielded significant plunder, success was far from guaranteed, and many buccaneers lived in poverty. Their ships were often small and poorly equipped compared to the heavily armed Spanish galleons they targeted. Nevertheless, the buccaneers' willingness to take extraordinary risks, coupled with their intimate knowledge of the Caribbean's waters, enabled them to outmaneuver and outfight larger and more powerful enemies.

The buccaneers' activities had profound consequences for the Caribbean. Their raids destabilized Spanish colonies, undermining Spain's economic and political control of the region. They also contributed to the growing perception of the Caribbean as a lawless and dangerous frontier, a place where the authority of empires was tenuous at best. Over time, the buccaneers' exploits became legendary, celebrated in both popular imagination and historical accounts.

The buccaneers of Hispaniola were more than just pirates; they were products of a specific historical moment, shaped by the unique conditions of the Caribbean. Their story is one of survival and adaptation, of marginalized individuals who found a way to thrive in a world defined by conflict and opportunity.

Port Royal: A Pirate Haven

Port Royal, Jamaica, was once the epicenter of Caribbean piracy, a thriving hub of trade, vice, and lawlessness that earned its infamous reputation as the "wickedest city on Earth." For decades, Port Royal stood as a testament to both the opportunities and the chaos of the pirate era, its prosperity fueled by plundered wealth and its downfall marked by catastrophic disaster.

Port Royal's transformation into a pirate haven began in the mid-17th century. In 1655, the English seized Jamaica from Spain during the Anglo-Spanish War, establishing a foothold in the Caribbean that would become crucial to their colonial ambitions. However, the island faced immediate challenges. Jamaica's economy was underdeveloped, its population was sparse, and it remained vulnerable to Spanish attempts at recapture. To bolster their position, the English authorities in Jamaica turned to privateers—state-sanctioned raiders who targeted Spanish ships and settlements.

Port Royal, with its deep natural harbor and strategic location at the entrance to Kingston Harbor, quickly became the base of operations for these privateers. The town offered easy access to the shipping lanes of the Spanish Main, making it an ideal staging ground for raids. Privateers such as Henry Morgan launched daring attacks from Port Royal, plundering Spanish wealth and delivering both spoils and protection to the fledgling English colony. These activities brought prosperity to Port Royal, transforming it into a bustling center of trade and commerce.

As privateering gave way to outright piracy, Port Royal embraced its role as a haven for pirates. By the late 17th century, the town had become a magnet for seafarers seeking refuge, adventure, and profit. Its streets were lined with taverns, brothels, and gambling dens, catering to the carousing lifestyles of its transient population. Merchants in Port Royal eagerly bought and sold goods stolen by pirates, creating a thriving black market economy. The town's wealth was reflected in its architecture, with grand houses and warehouses rising alongside its more infamous establishments.

Port Royal's reputation as a den of vice was well-deserved. Contemporary accounts describe it as a place of rampant debauchery, where wealth flowed freely and morality was in short supply. The pirate presence contributed to this lawlessness, as their ill-gotten riches fueled a culture of excess and hedonism. The town's inhabitants—an eclectic mix of pirates, merchants, sailors, and settlers—thrived in this environment, benefiting from the illicit trade that defined Port Royal's economy.

The prosperity of Port Royal, however, came at a cost. The town's dependence on piracy and its associated activities made it a target for criticism and retribution. European powers, particularly Spain, viewed Port Royal as a threat to their colonial interests, and its prominence drew the attention of the English Crown. As England sought to establish a more stable and legitimate colonial presence in the Caribbean, the tolerance for piracy waned.

Port Royal's decline was hastened by natural disaster. On June 7, 1692, a massive earthquake struck the town, causing much of it to collapse into the sea. The destruction was catastrophic, killing thousands and submerging large portions of Port Royal under water. The earthquake was seen by many contemporaries as divine punishment for the town's wickedness, a stark reminder of the fragility of its prosperity. While attempts were made to rebuild, Port Royal never regained its former prominence. Over time, it was eclipsed by Kingston, which became the new economic and political center of Jamaica.

Today, Port Royal exists as a shadow of its former self, a quiet fishing village far removed from its rowdy past.

The Spanish Main as a Target

The Spanish Main, a term broadly referring to Spain's mainland territories in the Americas, became the centerpiece of imperial wealth and a tantalizing target for pirates and privateers during the early modern period. Stretching along the northern coasts of South America and encompassing key ports and regions in Central America and the Caribbean, the Spanish Main was synonymous with the riches of the New World. The gold and silver extracted from mines in Peru and Mexico, transported across treacherous terrain and shipped through vulnerable ports, represented an irresistible prize for those willing to risk confrontation with the Spanish Empire.

The wealth of the Spanish Main stemmed largely from Spain's conquest of the Aztec and Inca empires. The treasures of these civilizations, including vast quantities of gold, silver, and precious stones, were systematically looted and transported to Spain via an intricate network of colonial ports and trade routes. Over time, this initial plunder gave way to the more industrialized extraction of resources. Mines like those at Potosí in present-day Bolivia and Zacatecas in Mexico became the economic lifeblood of the empire, producing unprecedented amounts of silver that fueled both Spain's global ambitions and the broader European economy.

The logistics of transporting these riches created significant vulnerabilities. Treasure from the interior of the Spanish colonies was carried to coastal ports such as Veracruz in Mexico and Nombre de Dios and Portobelo in Central America. From there, it was loaded onto heavily armed ships and organized into treasure fleets that sailed annually across the Atlantic to Spain. These fleets were escorted by military convoys, but the sheer scale of their cargo made them prime targets for raiders.

The Spanish Main's ports and trade routes were particularly vulnerable due to their geographic exposure and Spain's struggles to maintain effective colonial defenses. The Caribbean's many islands, hidden coves, and labyrinthine coastlines provided ideal staging grounds for attacks, allowing pirates and privateers to launch surprise raids and then disappear into the maze of waterways. Furthermore, the distances involved in maintaining colonial control stretched Spain's resources thin. Remote settlements often lacked sufficient fortifications or garrisons, making them easy prey for marauders.

The human element further exacerbated these vulnerabilities. Corruption, inefficiency, and internal rivalries plagued Spain's colonial administration. Officials tasked with protecting the colonies were often more concerned with enriching themselves than maintaining security. In some cases, local authorities even collaborated with pirates, selling them supplies or turning a blind eye to their activities in exchange for a share of the loot. This systemic weakness emboldened attackers, who recognized the limited capacity of the Spanish Empire to respond effectively.

The allure of the Spanish Main attracted a wide array of opportunists. Privateers operating under the flags of rival European powers such as England, France, and the Netherlands frequently targeted Spanish ships and settlements. Figures like Sir Francis Drake and Henry Morgan became infamous for their audacious raids on Spanish holdings, including the sacking of Nombre de Dios and the capture of Portobelo. These attacks dealt both economic and psychological blows to the Spanish Empire, undermining its claims to dominance in the Americas.

Independent pirates also thrived in the region, exploiting the wealth and weaknesses of the Spanish Main without the constraints of national allegiance. These raiders, often operating in small, fast ships, specialized in surprise attacks, ambushing merchant vessels and raiding lightly defended towns. Their ability to strike quickly and escape with their spoils made them a constant threat to Spanish shipping.

The impact of these attacks on the Spanish Main was profound. Beyond the immediate losses of treasure and resources, the raids disrupted trade, destabilized colonial economies, and exposed the limits of Spain's power in the Americas. The psychological toll was also significant; the constant threat of attack created an atmosphere of fear and insecurity among settlers and administrators alike. Over time, the sustained pressure from pirates and privateers contributed to the gradual erosion of Spain's dominance in the Caribbean.

Pirates of the Golden Age: Edward Mansvelt

His career exemplified the evolution of buccaneers from opportunistic raiders to organized and formidable maritime forces. While his life is not as well-documented as that of his successors, such as Henry Morgan, Mansvelt played a critical role in shaping the strategies and ambitions of Caribbean piracy during the mid-17th century. His exploits set the stage for the buccaneers' transformation into a unified and highly effective threat to Spanish dominance in the New World.

Mansvelt's origins remain largely mysterious, with scant information about his early life. He likely hailed from either England or the Netherlands, both of which provided a significant number of sailors to the buccaneering ranks. By the 1650s, Mansvelt had established himself as a prominent leader among the buccaneers, a diverse and loosely organized group of pirates and privateers who targeted Spanish ships and settlements throughout the Caribbean. These buccaneers operated with the tacit approval of rival European powers, particularly England and France, who sought to undermine Spain's control of the Americas.

Mansvelt's rise to prominence came as the buccaneers began to shift from small-scale raids to more ambitious and coordinated attacks. He was among the first to unite multiple pirate crews under a single command, creating a coalition capable of launching large-scale operations. This ability to organize disparate groups of buccaneers marked a turning point in the history of piracy, transforming what had been a loosely connected network of raiders into a cohesive and formidable force.

One of Mansvelt's most significant campaigns occurred in the early 1660s, when he led an expedition against the Spanish colony of Costa Rica. With a fleet of pirate ships and a sizable force of buccaneers, Mansvelt attacked San José, one of the region's key settlements. The raid, while ultimately unsuccessful in capturing the city, demonstrated the growing ambition and coordination of the buccaneers under Mansvelt's leadership. His ability to rally and command a diverse group of pirates set a precedent that would be followed by later figures, such as Henry Morgan.

Mansvelt's reputation as a leader extended beyond his military prowess. He was known for his ability to navigate the political complexities of the Caribbean, maintaining alliances with governors and colonial officials who benefited from the buccaneers' attacks on Spanish interests. These alliances provided Mansvelt and his crew with safe havens, supplies, and markets for their plunder, enabling them to sustain their operations over extended periods.

Despite his successes, Mansvelt's career was ultimately cut short. By the mid-1660s, his activities had drawn the ire of Spanish authorities, who viewed him as a significant threat to their colonies. Accounts of Mansvelt's fate vary. Some suggest he was captured by the Spanish and executed, while others imply he retired or disappeared. Regardless of the exact circumstances of his death, Mansvelt's influence on the buccaneers was profound. His leadership and organizational skills laid the groundwork for the later exploits of figures like Henry Morgan, who would build on Mansvelt's strategies to launch even more ambitious raids against the Spanish Empire.

Pirates of the Golden Age: Henry Morgan

Both celebrated and vilified, Morgan straddled the line between lawless pirate and legitimate privateer, operating with the blessing of the English Crown while engaging in acts of extraordinary brutality and plunder. His daring raids on Spanish colonies made him a hero in England and a villain in Spain, cementing his reputation as one of the most audacious and successful buccaneers of his time.

Born around 1635 in Llanrumney, Wales, Morgan's early life is shrouded in mystery. Some accounts suggest he was born into a modest farming family, while others speculate he came from a line of landed gentry. Little is known about his youth, but by the early 1650s, Morgan had made his way to the Caribbean, likely as an indentured servant. After serving his term, he entered the world of privateering—a legal form of piracy sanctioned during times of war—and began building his career as a seafaring adventurer.

Morgan's rise coincided with the growing rivalry between England and Spain for control of the Americas. By the mid-17th century, Spain's dominance in the Caribbean was under threat from other European powers, and England relied on privateers like Morgan to disrupt Spanish shipping and settlements. Operating under letters of marque issued by the governor of Jamaica, Morgan targeted Spanish colonies with both precision and ferocity, earning a reputation as a cunning strategist and ruthless leader.

One of Morgan's earliest and most famous exploits was the 1668 raid on Portobelo, a key Spanish port on the Isthmus of Panama. Leading a small fleet of buccaneers, Morgan launched a surprise attack, capturing the heavily fortified city and plundering its immense wealth. The raid not only demonstrated his military acumen but also exposed the vulnerabilities of Spanish defenses in the Caribbean. The success of the Portobelo raid brought Morgan widespread acclaim in Jamaica, where he was hailed as a patriot defending English interests against Spain.

Following this triumph, Morgan undertook a series of even more ambitious campaigns. In 1670, he set his sights on Panama City, the wealthiest Spanish settlement on the Pacific coast. To reach it, Morgan and his men crossed the Isthmus of Panama, enduring grueling conditions as they hacked through dense jungle. Despite being outnumbered,

Morgan's forces defeated the Spanish defenders and captured the city, which they looted extensively. The raid on Panama City was a staggering success, dealing a significant blow to Spanish prestige and enriching Morgan and his crew.

However, the raid also drew controversy. Morgan's actions violated a recently signed peace treaty between England and Spain, putting the English Crown in an awkward position. To defuse tensions, Morgan was arrested and sent to England, where he was expected to face punishment. Instead, he was treated as a hero. His exploits had made him a celebrity, and his actions were seen as part of England's broader effort to challenge Spanish dominance in the Americas. Rather than being punished, Morgan was knighted by King Charles II in 1674 and appointed Lieutenant Governor of Jamaica.

As Lieutenant Governor, Morgan took on the ironic role of suppressing piracy in the Caribbean, the very practice that had defined his career. While he was largely ineffective in this role, his position allowed him to retire comfortably, enjoying the wealth and status he had amassed. Morgan spent his later years as a plantation owner and prominent figure in Jamaican society. He died in 1688, likely from complications of alcohol-related illness, and was buried in Port Royal, the infamous pirate haven he had once called home.

Chapter 3: Pirate Tactics and Ships

The Ships of Fortune: Sloops and Brigs

The success of pirates during the Golden Age of Piracy owed as much to their choice of vessels as to their cunning and audacity. In the treacherous waters of the Caribbean, where quick strikes and rapid escapes were essential, speed and agility often determined a pirate's survival. Two types of ships, sloops and brigs, became indispensable tools of the trade. Their design, versatility, and performance allowed pirates to outmaneuver their prey, evade pursuers, and dominate the high seas.

The Caribbean presented unique challenges and opportunities for seafarers. Its waters were dotted with islands, reefs, and hidden coves, creating a labyrinthine geography ideal for ambushes and escapes. Pirates operating in this environment needed ships that could navigate shallow waters, sail close to the wind, and change course quickly. Sloops and brigs excelled in these conditions, giving pirates a significant tactical advantage over larger, less maneuverable vessels such as merchant ships and naval galleons.

Sloops, in particular, were prized for their exceptional speed and handling. Typically single-masted with a fore-and-aft rig, sloops were highly maneuverable and capable of sailing in almost any direction relative to the wind. This allowed pirates to chase down slower vessels or make swift retreats when threatened by superior forces. Sloops were also relatively small, making them difficult to spot and allowing them to navigate shallow coastal waters where larger ships could not follow. Their ability to dart in and out of hidden bays made them ideal for surprise attacks and ambushes, tactics that were central to pirate success.

Brigs, on the other hand, were larger and more heavily armed than sloops but retained much of their agility. These two-masted vessels, rigged with square sails, offered a balance between speed and firepower. Brigs could carry a substantial number of cannons, enabling pirates to engage in combat with merchant ships and even some smaller naval vessels. While not as nimble as sloops, brigs were fast enough to pursue prey and escape from danger, making them a popular choice for pirates who sought a more versatile ship.

The design of these ships also played a role in their effectiveness. Both sloops and brigs were built for efficiency, with sleek hulls that minimized drag and maximized speed. Their relatively small size made them easier to crew, an important consideration for pirates who often operated with limited manpower. The compact design of these vessels also meant that they could be easily modified to suit the needs of their captains. Pirates frequently stripped down their ships to reduce weight, added extra weaponry, or reinforced their decks to accommodate the spoils of their raids.

Pirates employed these ships in ways that exploited their strengths. Sloops, for example, were often used in hit-and-run attacks. A pirate crew aboard a sloop could approach a merchant vessel undetected, relying on their speed to close the distance quickly. Once alongside their target, they would launch a swift boarding attack, overwhelming the merchant crew before they had time to react. After seizing the cargo, the pirates could disappear into the maze of islands and inlets, their sloop outrunning any pursuers.

Brigs, with their greater firepower, were better suited for prolonged engagements. Pirate captains commanding brigs could intimidate their targets into surrendering without a fight, a tactic that minimized risk and ensured a higher chance of success. When combat was unavoidable, the brig's superior armament gave pirates a fighting chance against better-defended ships.

Pirates used their ships to evade the naval patrols dispatched to hunt them down. Larger, slower ships had little hope of catching a well-sailed sloop or brig, allowing pirates to operate with relative impunity. This advantage frustrated naval forces and merchant companies, who struggled to defend their interests against the swift and elusive sea raiders.

The choice of sloops and brigs also reflected the economic realities of piracy. Unlike naval forces, pirates lacked the resources to build or maintain large, heavily armed ships. Instead, they relied on capturing vessels from their victims, often targeting sloops and brigs because of their suitability for piracy. Once captured, these ships could be quickly adapted to the pirate's needs, creating a self-sustaining cycle that kept their fleets agile and effective.

Cannons, Swords, and Muskets

The weapons wielded by pirates during the Golden Age of Piracy were as essential to their survival as their ships. A pirate's arsenal, ranging from powerful cannons to close-combat swords and versatile muskets, was a key factor in their success on the high seas. These tools of war enabled pirates to overpower merchant ships, defend themselves against naval forces, and maintain discipline within their own ranks. Each weapon had a specific role, and their combined use often determined the outcome of a battle.

The most fearsome and decisive weapon in a pirate's arsenal was the cannon. Mounted on the decks of ships, cannons were used to disable enemy vessels, instill terror, and provide overwhelming firepower in combat. Cannons varied in size and type, but pirates generally favored smaller, more portable models like the swivel gun or the culverin, which were easier to maneuver on smaller vessels like sloops and brigs. These lighter cannons were particularly effective for their versatility, capable of firing solid shot to damage hulls, grapeshot to inflict maximum casualties on enemy crews, or chain shot to destroy sails and rigging, crippling a ship's ability to maneuver.

Cannons were often used not to sink a target but to intimidate and disable it. Pirates relied on their reputation for ferocity and ruthlessness to encourage their prey to surrender without a fight. A few well-placed shots from a cannon could create enough chaos to convince a merchant crew that resistance was futile. This strategy minimized damage to the ship and its cargo, which were the pirates' primary objectives. However, when a battle did occur, the roar of cannon fire and the smoke of gunpowder created a fearsome spectacle that highlighted the brutal realities of maritime warfare.

While cannons dominated long-range combat, swords were the weapon of choice for close-quarters fighting. Cutlasses, short and sturdy swords with curved blades, were particularly favored by pirates. Their compact size made them ideal for boarding actions, where the cramped conditions of a ship's deck demanded agility and precision. Cutlasses were also easy to wield and maintain, making them accessible to sailors with limited training in swordsmanship. In the heat of battle, these blades were used to slash, stab, and parry, their effectiveness amplified by the chaos and adrenaline of a boarding melee.

The psychological impact of the cutlass was nearly as important as its practical use. A pirate charging into battle, sword in hand, represented the raw aggression and fearlessness that defined their reputation. For many merchant crews, the sight of pirates armed with cutlasses and ready to board was enough to compel surrender. For pirates, this fear factor often ensured victory without the need for prolonged combat, reducing the risk of casualties and preserving their prize.

Muskets and pistols added another layer of lethality to a pirate's arsenal. These firearms were used both during boarding actions and in longer-range skirmishes, providing a versatile option for combat. Muskets, which fired a single lead ball or small shot, were effective at disabling enemy crew members and creating chaos on deck. Pirates often fired their muskets in volleys, maximizing their impact before closing the distance for hand-to-hand combat. While not as accurate or reliable as modern firearms, muskets were devastating in the close confines of a ship-to-ship engagement.

Pistols, smaller and easier to handle than muskets, were highly prized for their convenience and effectiveness in tight quarters. Pirates typically carried multiple pistols, often tucked into belts or sashes, allowing them to fire repeatedly without needing to reload—a crucial advantage in the chaos of battle. Flintlock pistols, the most common type, were notorious for their unpredictability but were nonetheless deadly at close range. A well-timed pistol shot could kill or incapacitate an opponent, turning the tide of a fight in an instant.

The combination of these weapons created a deadly toolkit that allowed pirates to dominate the high seas. However, these weapons were not without their limitations. Cannons required significant skill to operate effectively, and their ammunition and gunpowder were finite resources. Firearms were prone to misfires and malfunctions, especially in the humid and salty conditions of the Caribbean. Swords, while reliable, required physical strength and endurance to wield effectively in prolonged combat. Pirates had to adapt to these challenges, relying on ingenuity and teamwork to maximize the effectiveness of their arsenal.

Tactics of Terror and Strategy

Raiding was the cornerstone of pirate operations, a calculated act that blended stealth, speed, and brute force. Pirates typically targeted merchant ships, the lifeblood of colonial economies, which carried valuable commodities such as gold, silver, sugar, and spices. These ships were often poorly armed and crewed, making them ideal prey. Pirates relied on surprise to ensure their success, stalking their targets from a distance or lying in wait in secluded coves before launching their attacks. Timing was critical, as a well-executed raid could overwhelm a ship before its crew had the chance to organize a defense.

The geography of the Caribbean played a vital role in pirate raids. Its many islands, hidden bays, and narrow channels provided ideal cover for ambushes. Pirates used these natural features to their advantage, studying trade routes and the patterns of merchant shipping to identify vulnerable targets. They also took advantage of storms or other maritime hazards to mask their approach, striking when their prey was least prepared.

Once the target was within range, pirates would close in swiftly, using their nimble sloops or brigs to outmaneuver their often larger and slower adversaries. They would unleash a barrage of cannon fire, aimed not at sinking the ship but at crippling it. Chain shot and grapeshot were common munitions, designed to tear through sails, rigging, and crew rather than the hull. This tactic neutralized the target's ability to flee or defend itself, leaving it vulnerable to boarding.

Boarding was the decisive phase of a pirate attack, a chaotic and brutal melee where the outcome was often determined by speed and ferocity. Pirates would lash their ships to the target vessel, creating a bridge for their assault. Armed with cutlasses, pistols, and boarding axes, they would swarm aboard, overwhelming the enemy crew with sheer aggression. The confined space of a ship's deck favored the pirates, who thrived in close-quarters combat. Their ability to quickly subdue or neutralize resistance ensured that the plunder could be seized with minimal delay.

Pirates were not merely reliant on brute force; they were also adept practitioners of psychological warfare. Their reputation for ruthlessness and savagery often preceded them, creating an aura of fear that could paralyze their victims. The sight of a pirate ship flying the infamous Jolly Roger, a black flag emblazoned with symbols of death, was enough to compel many crews to surrender without a fight. This flag, and its variants, was a deliberate tool of intimidation, signaling that resistance would result in no quarter.

Captains like Blackbeard (Edward Teach) took psychological tactics to another level. Blackbeard famously tied slow-burning fuses into his beard, creating a terrifying image of smoke and fire that unnerved his enemies during boarding actions. Theatrics like these, combined with the sheer violence of pirate raids, created a legend of invincibility that pirates used to their advantage. Many merchant captains, faced with the choice between surrender and a potentially gruesome death, chose to hand over their cargo without resistance.

Pirates also manipulated their victims' fears by exploiting rumors and exaggerating their own ferocity. Stories of previous raids, often spread by survivors, amplified the terror associated with specific pirate crews or captains. This reputation for brutality, whether real or embellished, served as a powerful deterrent against resistance. For the pirates, it was a pragmatic strategy: the less they had to fight, the more efficient their operations became, reducing casualties and preserving their resources.

Beyond individual raids, pirates employed broader strategies to sustain their operations. They formed loose alliances with other pirate crews, creating networks that allowed them to share intelligence, resources, and safe havens. They also cultivated relationships with corrupt colonial officials or merchants, who provided supplies and markets for stolen goods in exchange for a share of the profits. These alliances and strategies enabled pirates to operate with relative impunity, evading capture and extending their reign over the seas.

The Jolly Roger: Under Crossbones

The origins of the term "Jolly Roger" are uncertain, but some scholars believe it may derive from the French term joli rouge ("pretty red"), referring to earlier red flags used to signal a ship's intention to fight to the death. Over time, black flags replaced red ones as the preferred symbol of piracy, likely because black was already associated with death and mourning. For pirates, a black flag signaled their identity and intent, a clear message that resistance would lead to destruction or no quarter—no mercy for the vanquished.

The most recognizable version of the Jolly Roger is the skull and crossbones, but this was just one of many designs employed by pirate captains. These flags were not standardized; instead, they were highly personalized, reflecting the individual personality and reputation of the pirate who commanded the ship. Each design served as a form of branding, reinforcing the pirate's fearsome image and spreading their notoriety.

Some pirate flags incorporated additional elements to amplify the threat. For example, the flag of Edward England featured a skull and crossbones above an hourglass, symbolizing the fleeting nature of life and the inevitability of death. Blackbeard's flag depicted a skeleton holding a spear in one hand and an hourglass in the other, while pointing at a bleeding heart—a grim reminder of the violence awaiting those who resisted. These macabre designs played on the superstitions and fears of sailors, making the flags an effective psychological weapon.

Other pirate captains used red flags, sometimes in combination with black. Known as the "Bloody Red," these flags were especially menacing, as they indicated that no mercy would be shown. A ship flying a red flag signaled an imminent attack in which the pirates intended to kill or capture everyone aboard, leaving no survivors. The mere sight of such a flag could demoralize a crew and lead to immediate surrender.

The Jolly Roger was not flown at all times. Pirates often approached their targets under false colors, hoisting the flag of a friendly or neutral nation to lull their prey into a false sense of security. Only when they were close enough to attack would they raise the black flag, revealing their true identity. This dramatic reveal was carefully timed to maximize the psychological impact, striking fear into the hearts of the merchant crew and encouraging them to surrender without a fight.

The symbolic power of the Jolly Roger was rooted in the reputation of pirates themselves. The flag was not merely a symbol of piracy; it was a promise of violence and death to anyone who resisted. The stories of atrocities committed by pirates, whether real or exaggerated, added to the flag's potency.

The effectiveness of the Jolly Roger lay in its ability to convey a clear and unambiguous message. It was a symbol of defiance against the established order, a declaration that pirates operated outside the laws of nations and would not be bound by them. At the same time, it was a practical tool that gave pirates a significant psychological advantage in their encounters with merchant ships and naval vessels.

Chapter 4: Life Aboard the Ship

Pirate Codes and Democracy

The image of pirates as unruly, chaotic rogues often obscures a surprising aspect of their existence: they operated under well-defined systems of governance. At a time when absolute monarchies and rigid hierarchies dominated the world, pirates embraced an early form of democracy that allowed them to function effectively in the unpredictable and dangerous environment of the high seas. Their self-governance was centered around "pirate codes," agreements that established rules and responsibilities for all members of a crew. These codes reflected the egalitarian values of pirate society while ensuring order and discipline in pursuit of shared goals.

Pirate codes, also known as articles of agreement, were written documents created and agreed upon by the crew of a pirate ship. These codes served as a social contract, outlining expectations for behavior, the distribution of plunder, and the resolution of disputes. While the specific terms varied from ship to ship, they all emphasized fairness, accountability, and collective decision-making, setting pirates apart from the rigid hierarchies of naval and merchant ships.

At the heart of pirate governance was the principle of shared decision-making. Key decisions, such as the election of the captain or whether to pursue a particular target, were made collectively by the crew. Captains, while often charismatic and skilled leaders, held their positions at the pleasure of the crew. If a captain failed to meet the crew's expectations or acted in a manner deemed tyrannical, he could be deposed and replaced through a vote. This system ensured that authority was earned through merit and trust rather than imposed by rank or privilege.

The quartermaster was another crucial figure in pirate governance, acting as a counterbalance to the captain's authority. Elected by the crew, the quartermaster oversaw the division of plunder, maintained discipline, and represented the interests of the crew in disputes. In battle, the quartermaster played a critical role in organizing the crew and ensuring that the ship operated efficiently. The position was highly respected, as the quartermaster often served as a mediator and protector of the crew's rights.

One of the most important aspects of pirate codes was their emphasis on equality, particularly in the distribution of wealth. Unlike naval or merchant ships, where officers and owners claimed the lion's share of profits, pirate crews divided their spoils according to agreed-upon shares. The captain and quartermaster typically received larger portions, reflecting their leadership roles, but the rest of the crew shared equally in the plunder. This system of equitable distribution fostered a sense of camaraderie and mutual investment in the success of their ventures.

Discipline and order were also key components of pirate codes. While pirates were known for their debauchery and violence, they understood the necessity of maintaining order aboard ship. The codes outlined punishments for infractions such as theft, desertion, or insubordination. Penalties ranged from fines and reduced shares to more severe consequences, such as marooning or execution, for those who endangered the crew or undermined its cohesion. These rules ensured that the ship operated efficiently and minimized internal conflict, which could be disastrous in the high-stakes world of piracy.

The democratic nature of pirate governance extended beyond the ship itself. Pirate communities, particularly those in havens like Nassau in the Bahamas or Tortuga off the coast of Hispaniola, often mirrored the egalitarian principles of their ships. These havens provided pirates with a degree of freedom and autonomy unavailable in colonial societies, allowing them to create communities where decisions were made collectively, and resources were shared. This freedom attracted individuals from diverse backgrounds, including escaped slaves, marginalized settlers, and adventurers, further reinforcing the ethos of pirate society.

The pirate codes and their emphasis on democracy were born out of necessity as much as ideology. The harsh and unpredictable life of a pirate required a system that balanced individual freedoms with collective responsibility. By creating rules that promoted fairness and accountability, pirates ensured the survival and success of their crews in an environment where external authority was absent.

Roles and Hierarchies: From captains to powder monkeys

Unlike the rigid hierarchies of naval or merchant ships, pirate crews often prided themselves on a more democratic structure, but this did not mean the absence of rank or responsibility. Roles aboard a pirate vessel were well-defined, with each position serving a crucial function in maintaining order, ensuring efficiency, and achieving success in raids and battles.

At the top of the hierarchy was the captain, the most prominent and powerful figure aboard the ship. Unlike in naval fleets, where captains were appointed by royal decree, pirate captains were elected by the crew, and their authority was conditional on maintaining the trust and respect of their peers. A pirate captain's primary role was to lead during combat and make strategic decisions, such as selecting targets or navigating treacherous waters. Charisma, bravery, and cunning were essential qualities for a captain, as the position required the ability to inspire loyalty and confidence in the crew. However, the captain's power was not absolute. If the crew became dissatisfied with their leader, they could vote to depose and replace them, ensuring that authority remained accountable.

Second in command was the quartermaster, a figure almost as influential as the captain. The quartermaster was responsible for enforcing discipline, dividing plunder, and representing the interests of the crew in decision-making. In many ways, the quartermaster acted as a check on the captain's power, ensuring that no single individual could dominate the crew. During battles, the quartermaster took on a leadership role, often directing boarding actions and ensuring the efficient use of resources. The position required a combination of organizational skills, fairness, and a reputation for toughness, as the quartermaster was often tasked with meting out punishments for violations of the pirate code.

Below the quartermaster, other officers played specialized roles crucial to the ship's operation. The boatswain oversaw the maintenance of the ship and its equipment, ensuring that sails, rigging, and hull were in good condition. The gunner was in charge of the ship's artillery, responsible for maintaining cannons, storing gunpowder, and training the crew in their use. The navigator, or sailing master, was tasked with plotting the ship's course and ensuring that it reached its destinations safely. Navigators often held unique status aboard pirate ships due to the specialized knowledge required for their role. While they were not always pirates themselves—many were captured from merchant or naval vessels—their skills were indispensable.

The surgeon, if a ship was fortunate enough to have one, was responsible for tending to the crew's medical needs. Surgeons faced the grim reality of treating injuries sustained in battle, amputating limbs, and combating diseases like scurvy or dysentery. They were often regarded with a mix of respect and fear, as their crude methods could mean the difference between life and death. In the absence of a trained surgeon, the carpenter sometimes assumed this role, using their tools and skills to perform makeshift medical procedures.

Ordinary crew members, known as seamen or sailors, formed the backbone of the pirate ship. They handled the day-to-day tasks of sailing, such as manning the rigging, steering, and maintaining the ship's cleanliness. These men were also the primary combatants during raids and boarding actions, wielding cutlasses, pistols, and muskets with deadly intent. While their roles were less glamorous than those of officers, their contributions were vital to the success of the ship's operations.

Among the youngest and most vulnerable members of the crew were the powder monkeys, typically boys or very young men. Their role was to ferry gunpowder from the ship's magazine to the cannons during battle, a perilous task that required speed and agility. Powder monkeys were often recruited—or forcibly taken—from ports and coastal towns, drawn into piracy at a young age. Despite their low rank, their work was critical to the ship's firepower and overall survival in combat.

Life aboard a pirate ship was demanding and dangerous, with every member of the crew exposed to the hardships of the sea and the risks of battle. Yet, the roles and hierarchies aboard pirate vessels reflected a pragmatic approach to governance. Each role was necessary, and the distribution of responsibilities allowed the ship to function as a cohesive unit. Unlike in naval or merchant vessels, where rank often dictated privilege, pirate crews emphasized fairness, particularly in the division of plunder. Shares were distributed according to rank and contribution, but even the lowest-ranking crew members were guaranteed a portion of the spoils, reinforcing the sense of shared purpose that was essential to pirate life.

The Harsh Realities

Life aboard a pirate ship, despite its romanticized depiction in popular culture, was harsh, unforgiving, and fraught with dangers beyond the perils of battle. Pirates faced not only the threat of violent confrontations at sea but also the relentless hardships of disease, injuries, and brutal disciplinary measures.

Disease was one of the greatest threats to a pirate crew, as it was for all seafarers of the time. The close quarters of a ship, combined with poor sanitation and limited medical knowledge, created the perfect breeding ground for illnesses. Scurvy, caused by a deficiency of vitamin C, was particularly common. It weakened the body, causing swollen gums, open sores, and eventually death if untreated. Pirates, like other sailors, were often malnourished, surviving on a diet of salted meat, hardtack, and whatever provisions they could steal or forage. The lack of fresh fruits and vegetables made scurvy an ever-present danger.

Other diseases, such as dysentery, typhus, and malaria, also ravaged pirate crews. Contaminated water supplies and unsanitary conditions contributed to outbreaks of illness, which could decimate a ship's crew and render it vulnerable to attack. The tropical climates where many pirates operated further exposed them to mosquito-borne diseases like malaria and yellow fever, which could spread rapidly and with devastating effects. Without effective treatments, many pirates succumbed to these illnesses, leaving the survivors to navigate both their grief and the practical challenges of operating a ship with a diminished crew.

Battles at sea were brutal and chaotic, with pirates facing the constant risk of being maimed or killed. Cannon fire, musket shots, and sword wounds were common during raids and boarding actions. The confined space of a ship's deck often turned combat into a bloody melee, where even minor injuries could prove fatal if they became infected. Amputations were a grim but necessary procedure for treating severe wounds. Surgeons, if available, used rudimentary tools and minimal anesthesia—often just rum or brute restraint—to perform these operations, leaving many pirates permanently disabled.

Even outside of combat, the ship itself posed dangers. The daily tasks of sailing required physical exertion and carried significant risks. Crew members could fall from rigging, be swept overboard during storms, or suffer injuries from handling heavy equipment. In such cases, the lack of advanced medical care meant that even seemingly minor accidents could result in death or long-term disability.

Punishment aboard pirate ships, while often less arbitrary than on naval or merchant vessels, was nonetheless severe when rules were broken. The pirate code, which governed life on many ships, set clear expectations for behavior and outlined penalties for infractions. Theft, desertion, and disobedience were among the most serious offenses, as they threatened the cohesion and survival of the crew. Punishments were designed to maintain discipline and deter further violations, but they were also brutal reminders of the high stakes of pirate life.

One of the most feared punishments was marooning, in which a crew member was abandoned on a deserted island or remote shore with minimal supplies. This sentence was typically reserved for acts of treachery or mutiny, leaving the condemned to face a slow death from starvation, exposure, or wild animals. Another common punishment was flogging, where the offender was whipped with a cat-o'-nine-tails, a multi-tailed whip designed to inflict maximum pain. While flogging was less severe than marooning, it left lasting scars and served as a public display of the consequences of breaking the code.

Keelhauling, though less frequently practiced, was one of the most gruesome punishments associated with piracy. The offender was tied to a rope and dragged under the ship's hull, where sharp barnacles could tear their flesh. This punishment was often fatal and was intended as a horrifying deterrent. Pirates were also known to administer lesser punishments, such as confinement or reduced shares of plunder, for minor offenses.

The Spoils of Victory

For pirates, the promise of plunder was the ultimate incentive for enduring the hardships of life at sea. Every raid, battle, and act of piracy was driven by the allure of treasure—gold, silver, jewels, and other valuables that could transform the lives of those who risked everything to obtain them.

Typically, the captain received a larger share of the loot, reflecting their leadership role and the responsibilities of guiding the ship through dangerous waters and battles. The quartermaster, who acted as a mediator and enforcer of the pirate code, also received an enhanced portion. However, even the lowest-ranking members of the crew, such as sailors and powder monkeys, were guaranteed a fair share of the spoils. This system stood in stark contrast to the rigid hierarchies of the time, where wealth was often concentrated in the hands of a few. It was designed to maintain morale and ensure that every crew member felt invested in the success of their ventures.

The division process itself was a highly organized affair. After a successful raid, the crew gathered to catalog and appraise the captured goods. Items of immediate use, such as weapons, ammunition, or medical supplies, were set aside for the ship's operation. The remaining plunder, which could include coins, precious metals, fine textiles, spices, and other valuables, was divided into shares according to the agreed-upon rules. This transparency ensured that disputes were minimized and that trust among the crew was maintained.

Once the shares were distributed, many pirates turned their attention to life on land, where they could enjoy the fruits of their labor. Port towns like Port Royal in Jamaica, Tortuga off the coast of Hispaniola, and Nassau in the Bahamas became notorious hubs for pirates looking to spend their earnings. These towns offered a mix of debauchery, entertainment, and commerce, providing everything a pirate could desire: rum, gambling, women, and fine goods. Taverns and brothels thrived on pirate wealth, and the influx of plundered riches often created local economies dependent on piracy.

For many pirates, these periods on land represented a rare opportunity for indulgence and respite from the dangers of the sea. They spent lavishly, often squandering their earnings in a matter of weeks or months. This extravagance was partly fueled by the unpredictability of pirate life. Few pirates expected to survive long enough to save for the future, so they embraced the philosophy of living for the moment, enjoying their wealth while they could.

However, not all pirates squandered their plunder. Some sought to use their earnings to escape the perilous life of piracy. A few invested in legitimate businesses, purchased property, or settled in remote colonies where they could start anew. Others attempted to launder their ill-gotten gains through merchants or corrupt officials, blending into society as wealthy traders or landowners. These individuals often faced challenges in shedding their pirate identities, as their wealth and reputations sometimes attracted unwanted attention from authorities or rivals. Wealthy pirates became targets for betrayal and violence, both from within their own ranks and from outsiders looking to claim a share of the riches. On land, they were vulnerable to arrest or capture by colonial authorities, particularly as governments began cracking down on piracy in the late 17th and early 18th centuries. For many pirates, the fleeting pleasures of land-based indulgence were overshadowed by the constant threat of discovery and punishment.

Chapter 5: The Legends of the Sea

Francis Drake

Francis Drake, one of the most renowned figures in maritime history, was a skilled navigator, privateer, explorer, and one of England's greatest national heroes. Francis Drake was born around 1540 in Tavistock, Devon, England, into a family of modest means. As the eldest of twelve children, he grew up near the sea, where he developed a fascination with maritime life. Apprenticed to a merchant shipmaster, Drake learned the fundamentals of navigation and seamanship. By his early twenties, he had already begun his career as a mariner, sailing to the Americas and participating in early English expeditions.

Drake's first major ventures into piracy occurred during his association with his cousin John Hawkins, a prominent seafarer. Together, they engaged in voyages to the West Indies, combining trade with illicit activities such as attacking Spanish settlements and vessels. These early encounters with the Spanish were formative for Drake, exposing him to the wealth of the Spanish Empire and the vulnerabilities of its colonial holdings.

Drake's fame soared during his circumnavigation of the globe between 1577 and 1580, a journey that cemented his place in history. Commissioned by Queen Elizabeth I, Drake set sail aboard the Golden Hind with the dual purpose of exploring new trade routes and harassing Spanish interests. Along the way, he plundered Spanish ports in South America, captured treasure-laden ships, and navigated uncharted waters. His most famous prize was the Nuestra Señora de la Concepción, a Spanish galleon loaded with gold, silver, and precious stones. The voyage was a resounding success, and upon his return to England, Drake was hailed as a hero and knighted by the Queen.

Drake's exploits did more than enrich himself and his crew; they dealt a significant blow to Spain's economy and colonial ambitions. His circumnavigation demonstrated England's growing naval capabilities and marked the nation's entry into the global stage as a maritime power. However, Spain viewed Drake's actions as acts of piracy, deepening the rivalry between the two nations and setting the stage for future conflicts.

Drake's reputation as a fearless privateer continued to grow in the 1580s. He launched raids on Spanish colonies in the Americas, including a devastating attack on the port of Cartagena. He also disrupted Spain's treasure fleets, capturing vast quantities of gold and silver. These attacks, conducted under the authority of Queen Elizabeth I, blurred the lines between legitimate privateering and piracy. While England celebrated his victories, Spain regarded him as a criminal and placed a hefty bounty on his head.

Drake's most famous military achievement came in 1588 during the conflict with the Spanish Armada. As vice admiral of the English fleet, he played a crucial role in the defeat of the Armada, a turning point in European history.

His leadership, combined with his knowledge of naval tactics and his ability to inspire his men, helped secure England's naval supremacy. The victory not only thwarted Spain's invasion plans but also marked the beginning of England's dominance on the seas.

Despite his many successes, Drake's later years were marked by setbacks. In 1595, he led an expedition to the Caribbean alongside Sir John Hawkins, aiming to capture Spanish treasure ships and settlements. The campaign ended in failure, with both men succumbing to illness. Drake died of dysentery on January 28, 1596, off the coast of Panama. He was buried at sea, his body placed in a lead coffin and lowered into the waters near Portobelo, a fitting end for a man whose life was defined by the sea.

François l'Olonnais

His reign of terror marked him as a notorious figure in the annals of piracy, a man whose ruthlessness earned him both infamy and a reputation as one of the most savage buccaneers of his era. Operating primarily in the Spanish Main, l'Olonnais became a symbol of the lawlessness and violence that defined the buccaneering period.

L'Olonnais began his maritime career as an indentured servant, traveling to the French colonies in the Americas. By the early 1660s, he had completed his term of servitude and joined the buccaneers—pirates and privateers who operated out of Tortuga, a notorious haven off the coast of Hispaniola. Tortuga was home to a diverse and dangerous community of seafarers who targeted Spanish ships and settlements, challenging Spain's dominance in the

Caribbean. L'Olonnais quickly proved himself among these ranks, displaying a combination of cunning, ambition, and ruthlessness that set him apart.

His first major successes came through privateering, where he attacked Spanish vessels under the tacit approval of French colonial authorities. However, l'Olonnais's activities soon crossed the line into outright piracy. His hatred for the Spanish, reportedly fueled by harsh treatment he endured at their hands earlier in his life, drove him to extremes of violence. He became known for his willingness to torture captives to extract information about hidden treasure or strategic defenses. Tales of his brutality spread quickly, with reports of l'Olonnais beheading entire crews or cutting out prisoners' tongues to intimidate his enemies.

In one of his most infamous exploits, l'Olonnais captured a Spanish ship near the coast of Cuba. After defeating the crew, he slaughtered most of them and sent one survivor back to the Spanish authorities with a grim message: a declaration of his intent to continue attacking Spanish interests with unrelenting vengeance. This act of calculated terror heightened his reputation as a pirate who showed no mercy, instilling fear in his enemies and ensuring that his name would not be forgotten.

L'Olonnais's boldest campaigns involved raids on the Spanish Main, where he targeted settlements and treasure-laden ships. One of his most significant achievements was the sack of Maracaibo, a wealthy Spanish city in present-day Venezuela. In 1666, leading a fleet of buccaneers, he attacked the town, looting its riches and torturing its inhabitants to reveal hidden wealth. From there, he continued to ravage the surrounding region, leaving a trail of destruction and horror in his wake. These raids solidified his place as one of the most successful and feared buccaneers of his time.

Despite his successes, l'Olonnais's career was marked by growing recklessness and diminishing returns. His extreme cruelty, while effective in some instances, earned him the enmity of not only the Spanish but also other powers in the region. By the late 1660s, his fortunes began to decline. In one disastrous expedition, l'Olonnais attempted to raid Nicaragua, but his fleet was shipwrecked off the coast of Central America. Stranded and desperate, he and his crew resorted to cannibalism to survive, an act that added another dark layer to his legend.

L'Olonnais's downfall came not long after. In 1668, while attempting to lead a new raid, he was captured by indigenous people in the Darién region of present-day Panama. According to accounts, the natives, who had suffered greatly at the hands of pirates and European colonizers, executed l'Olonnais with brutal finality. Some stories claim he was dismembered alive and his body burned—a fittingly gruesome end for a man whose life had been defined by violence.

Bartholomew Sharp

Active in the late 17th century, Sharp is best remembered for his audacious raids along the Pacific coast of Central and South America, an area that was largely inaccessible to European pirates. His ability to outmaneuver Spanish forces, combined with his remarkable navigation skills, made him one of the most notable pirates of his time.

Little is known about Sharp's early life, but he first emerged in historical records as part of a crew of buccaneers operating in the Caribbean in the 1670s. In 1679, he joined an ambitious expedition to raid Spanish settlements and ships in the Pacific Ocean. The plan required a daring journey across the Isthmus of Panama, where the crew carried their small boats through the dense jungle to reach the Pacific. This feat alone was a testament to the determination and resourcefulness of the buccaneers.

Once in the Pacific, Sharp and his companions launched a campaign of plunder that terrorized Spanish settlements along the coasts of modern-day Panama, Ecuador, Peru, and Chile. Their activities disrupted trade routes and alarmed colonial authorities, who struggled to mount an effective defense against the agile and unpredictable pirates. Sharp's ability to navigate unfamiliar waters played a crucial role in their success, allowing the buccaneers to evade pursuit and strike at vulnerable targets.

One of Sharp's most significant achievements was his leadership of the Trinity, a captured Spanish ship that became the flagship of the expedition. Under his command, the Trinity became a symbol of pirate dominance in the Pacific, successfully engaging larger and better-armed Spanish vessels. Sharp's tactical brilliance and charismatic leadership earned him the loyalty of his crew, even as the hardships of the voyage tested their resolve.

Sharp's most famous exploit occurred in 1681 when he captured a Spanish treasure galleon carrying a trove of gold, silver, and precious gems. The success of this raid cemented his reputation as a masterful pirate and a thorn in the side of the Spanish Empire. However, as with many pirate ventures, internal disputes among the crew threatened to undermine their success. Sharp's leadership was challenged, and a faction of the crew eventually mutinied, leaving him in command of a reduced force.

Faced with dwindling resources and mounting Spanish resistance, Sharp made the decision to return to the Atlantic. Navigating through dangerous waters, Sharp and his crew charted new routes, producing a detailed map of the Pacific coast that would later prove invaluable to European powers seeking to challenge Spanish dominance in the region. The map, often referred to as the "South Sea Waggoner," was presented to the English Crown, earning Sharp a royal pardon and transforming him from an outlaw into a celebrated navigator.

Blackbeard: The Fearsome Icon

Edward Teach, better known as Blackbeard, stands as one of the most infamous figures in the history of piracy. His larger-than-life persona, crafted through a combination of calculated theatrics and ruthless actions, has immortalized him as a fearsome icon of the Golden Age of Piracy. Active during the early 18th century, Blackbeard's brief but impactful reign of terror left an indelible mark on the seas and in the annals of maritime history.

Little is known about Blackbeard's early life, including his exact birthdate and place, though it is widely believed he was born around 1680 in Bristol, England. Originally a sailor in privateering ventures during Queen Anne's War (1702–1713), Teach turned to piracy after the conflict ended, like many others who found themselves unemployed and adrift. By the time he adopted the moniker Blackbeard, he had already begun building a reputation as a cunning and formidable pirate.

Blackbeard's rise to prominence began in 1717 when he captured the French slave ship La Concorde. Renaming it Queen Anne's Revenge, he transformed the vessel into a heavily armed warship, mounting 40 guns and manning it with a large crew. With this formidable flagship, Blackbeard terrorized the waters of the Caribbean and along the American coast, targeting merchant vessels and occasionally blockading entire ports.

What set Blackbeard apart from other pirates was not just his ability to capture ships but his mastery of psychological warfare. He cultivated an image designed to instill fear in his enemies. Teach was described as a towering figure with a wild, unkempt beard from which he derived his infamous nickname. To enhance his terrifying appearance, he would tie slow-burning fuses into his beard and beneath his hat during battles, creating an aura of smoke and fire that gave him a demonic visage. The sight of Blackbeard charging into battle with his smoldering beard and ferocious demeanor was enough to cause many opponents to surrender without a fight.

Blackbeard's exploits became legendary, particularly his audacious blockade of the port of Charleston, South Carolina, in May 1718. Leading a small fleet, he captured several ships and held prominent citizens hostage, demanding a chest of medical supplies as ransom. The blockade was a strategic masterstroke, showcasing his ability to control major shipping routes and strike fear into colonial authorities. After receiving the ransom, Blackbeard released his prisoners and disappeared into the vastness of the Atlantic, leaving chaos in his wake.

Despite his reputation for violence, Blackbeard was also known as a shrewd and pragmatic leader. He often avoided unnecessary bloodshed, relying instead on his fearsome image to secure compliance. When force was required, however, he wielded it with devastating effect, ensuring that his legend grew with each encounter.

In June 1718, Blackbeard negotiated a royal pardon in Bath, North Carolina, as part of a broader effort by colonial authorities to suppress piracy. However, the allure of plunder proved too strong, and he soon returned to his old ways. This defiance made him a target for the British Navy, which intensified its efforts to eliminate him.

Blackbeard's reign of terror came to a dramatic end on November 22, 1718, during a fierce battle off the coast of Ocracoke Island, North Carolina. Lieutenant Robert Maynard of the British Royal Navy, commanding the HMS Pearl, engaged Blackbeard in a bloody fight. Despite being outnumbered, Blackbeard fought with characteristic ferocity, reportedly sustaining over 20 wounds, including five gunshot wounds, before being killed. His severed head was mounted on the bow of Maynard's ship as a grim warning to other pirates.

Blackbeard's death marked the end of one of piracy's most notorious careers, but his legend only grew in the centuries that followed. Stories of his exploits, both real and embellished, became a cornerstone of pirate lore, inspiring countless books, films, and popular culture representations. To this day, Blackbeard remains a symbol of the audacious, larger-than-life figure that defined the Golden Age of Piracy.

Anne Bonny and Mary Read

Anne Bonny and Mary Read stand out in the history of piracy as extraordinary figures who defied the rigid gender norms of the 18th century. In a world dominated by men, where women were often excluded from seafaring life and seen as bad luck aboard ships, Bonny and Read shattered conventions by becoming notorious pirates.

Anne Bonny was born in County Cork, Ireland, around 1700, the illegitimate daughter of a prominent lawyer and his servant. Her father, seeking to escape scandal, relocated the family to the American colonies, settling in Charleston, South Carolina. Anne grew up with a fiery temperament, reportedly stabbing a servant in anger and rejecting the traditional domestic roles expected of women. Her defiance of societal norms became evident when she married a small-time sailor, James Bonny, against her father's wishes, severing ties with her family and their wealth.

Anne's life changed dramatically after her marriage. Disillusioned with her husband, who reportedly became an informant for the governor of the Bahamas, she found herself drawn to the pirate community in Nassau, a haven for outlaws. There she met the charismatic pirate captain John "Calico Jack" Rackham and began an affair with him. Anne joined Rackham's crew, disguising herself as a man to fit in among the pirates. Her ability to fight alongside her male counterparts and her unwavering loyalty to Rackham quickly earned her a place among the crew.

Mary Read's story was equally unconventional. Born in England around 1690, she was disguised as a boy by her widowed mother to claim financial support from her deceased husband's family. Read continued to live as a man into adulthood, serving in the British military and distinguishing herself in battle. After leaving the army, she sought work on merchant ships and eventually turned to piracy. Like Anne Bonny, Mary joined Rackham's crew, hiding her true identity from most of her shipmates.

The paths of Anne Bonny and Mary Read converged aboard Rackham's ship, where the two formed a close bond. Both women proved themselves as formidable fighters, participating in raids and battles with ferocity that rivaled their male counterparts. Accounts suggest they fought with pistols and cutlasses, often leading charges during boarding actions. Their bravery and skill earned them the respect of their crew, despite the deep-seated prejudices of the time.

Their partnership with Rackham's crew became legendary, but it also marked the beginning of their downfall. In

October 1720, their ship was captured by a pirate-hunting sloop under the command of Captain Jonathan Barnet, sent by the Governor of Jamaica. During the battle, Rackham and most of his crew were too drunk to fight effectively. Bonny and Read, however, stood their ground, reportedly being the last to surrender.

Following their capture, Rackham and the male members of the crew were tried and executed for piracy. Anne Bonny and Mary Read were also sentenced to death but managed to delay their executions by pleading pregnancy—a legal loophole known as "pleading the belly." Mary Read died in prison shortly afterward, likely from fever, before her sentence could be carried out. Anne Bonny's fate remains uncertain. Some accounts suggest she was eventually released, possibly through the intervention of her influential father, and lived out her life in obscurity.

The stories of Anne Bonny and Mary Read have been romanticized over the centuries, but their significance extends beyond their individual exploits. As women who dared to live on their own terms in an era that offered them little agency, they challenged societal norms and demonstrated that courage and determination were not limited by gender.

"Black Bart" Roberts

Bartholomew Roberts, better known as "Black Bart," holds the distinction of being the most successful pirate in history by the sheer number of prizes he captured. Over the course of a brief but extraordinary career from 1719 to 1722, Roberts is estimated to have seized more than 400 ships, a record unmatched by any of his contemporaries. His combination of daring, discipline, and tactical brilliance made him a legend of the Golden Age of Piracy, transforming him from an unwilling participant in piracy to one of its most iconic figures.

Roberts was born John Roberts around 1682 in Casnewydd-Bach, Wales, a small village near modern-day Pembrokeshire. Before his life of piracy, he worked as a merchant sailor, a career that gave him extensive knowledge of navigation and the workings of ships. In 1719, Roberts was serving as a mate aboard the Princess, a slaving vessel, when it was captured by pirates under the command of Howell Davis off the coast of West Africa. Initially a reluctant recruit, Roberts soon adapted to his new life, impressing Davis with his skills and intelligence. When Davis was killed in an ambush, the crew elected Roberts as their captain—a decision that would change the course of piracy history.

Roberts embraced his role with unexpected zeal, transforming his crew into a disciplined and formidable force. Unlike many pirates of his era, Roberts demanded order and maintained strict rules aboard his ships. He enforced a pirate code that prohibited drunkenness during battle, encouraged cleanliness, and required fair distribution of plunder. His leadership style won the respect of his crew, who valued his strategic acumen and boldness.

One of Roberts's earliest triumphs was the capture of a fleet of Portuguese ships near the island of Principe. Among the vessels was a richly laden treasure ship carrying gold and other valuables. This windfall solidified Roberts's reputation and demonstrated his ability to outwit and overpower his targets. He began flying his infamous flag, which depicted a figure holding an hourglass and a flaming sword, symbolizing both the fleeting nature of life and the deadly consequences of resistance.

Roberts's operations spanned vast areas, including the coasts of West Africa, the Caribbean, and even the North American colonies. He was known for his audacious tactics, often attacking heavily defended convoys and coastal settlements with overwhelming force. In one of his most famous exploits, Roberts blockaded the port of Trepassey in Newfoundland, capturing or destroying 22 ships and humiliating the local authorities by forcing their crews to surrender without a fight.

Another celebrated success came in the Caribbean, where Roberts seized the Onslow, a Royal Navy frigate. This daring act not only provided him with a powerful new flagship, renamed the Royal Fortune, but also dealt a blow to the morale of naval forces tasked with suppressing piracy. Roberts's ability to capture military vessels demonstrated his tactical brilliance and underscored the weaknesses of the anti-piracy efforts of the time.

Roberts was not only a master of naval combat but also a shrewd psychological tactician. He understood the importance of fear in pirate operations and cultivated a fearsome reputation that often led his targets to surrender without resistance. The sight of his flag or the approach of his fleet was enough to strike terror into the hearts of merchant crews, who knew that defiance could mean death or destruction.

Despite his unparalleled success, Roberts's career was cut short in February 1722 when his ship was intercepted by the Royal Navy frigate HMS Swallow near Cape Lopez, off the coast of Gabon. During the ensuing battle, Roberts was struck by grapeshot and killed instantly. His crew, unwilling to allow his body to be taken as a trophy, wrapped it in a sail and buried it at sea. The loss of their leader demoralized the crew, many of whom were captured and later executed in what became one of the largest anti-piracy trials of the era.

The Mysterious Captain Kidd

Captain William Kidd is one of the most enigmatic figures in the history of piracy, remembered as both a notorious pirate and a victim of political intrigue. His story, shrouded in mystery and contradiction, has sparked debates over whether he was truly a villainous pirate or an unwitting scapegoat caught in the turbulent politics of the late 17th century.

William Kidd was born around 1654 in Dundee, Scotland. Little is known about his early life, but he likely went to sea as a young man, working his way up to become a skilled mariner. By the 1680s, Kidd had settled in New York City, where he married and became a respected member of the community. His reputation as a capable and reliable sailor earned him the attention of influential figures in colonial and English government, setting the stage for his controversial career.

Kidd's entry into the world of privateering—a legal form of state-sanctioned piracy—came in 1695. England was at war with France, and privateers were authorized to attack enemy ships and plunder their cargo. Kidd was commissioned by a group of prominent investors, including members of the English aristocracy, to command a privateering mission against French vessels and pirates operating in the Indian Ocean. Backed by a letter of marque, Kidd set sail in the Adventure Galley, a well-armed ship designed for speed and combat.

What began as a legitimate privateering mission quickly unraveled into a series of controversial incidents. Kidd's commission required him to target only enemy ships, but the complex and overlapping jurisdictions of maritime law often made it difficult to determine the legitimacy of a prize. In 1698, Kidd captured the Quedagh Merchant, a richly laden Armenian ship sailing under French passes. While Kidd claimed the ship was a legitimate target, his critics argued that it was under the protection of the East India Company, making its seizure an act of piracy.

The Quedagh Merchant episode marked the turning point in Kidd's fortunes. Reports of his actions reached England, where powerful political rivals sought to discredit him and his backers. Kidd, now labeled a pirate, became the subject of a manhunt. Unaware of the full extent of the accusations against him, he returned to the Caribbean, where he attempted to clear his name by negotiating with colonial authorities. Eventually, he sailed to Boston, hoping to secure a pardon from Governor Richard Coote, Earl of Bellomont, one of his original sponsors.

Instead of receiving a pardon, Kidd was arrested and sent to England for trial. His trial in 1701 was a highly politicized affair, with Kidd painted as a ruthless pirate despite his protests of innocence. He was charged with piracy and the murder of a crew member, William Moore, whom Kidd had struck with a heavy bucket during a quarrel. The court found Kidd guilty on both counts, and he was executed by hanging. His body was then gibbeted—displayed in chains along the Thames River—as a grim warning to others who might turn to piracy.

The ambiguity of Kidd's story has fueled centuries of speculation. Some historians argue that Kidd was a victim of circumstance, betrayed by political rivals and punished to appease the East India Company, which wielded immense influence. Others contend that Kidd knowingly crossed the line into piracy, motivated by the immense wealth he stood to gain.

Adding to Kidd's mystique is the legend of his buried treasure. Before his arrest, Kidd is rumored to have hidden a portion of his plunder on Gardiners Island, off the coast of New York. While some of this treasure was recovered and presented as evidence at his trial, the idea that Kidd left behind a vast, undiscovered fortune has captured the imagination of treasure hunters and storytellers alike.

Charles Vane, "The Rebel Pirate"

Known for his defiance of authority and his ruthless tactics, Vane embodied the rebellious spirit that defined piracy during its peak in the early 18th century. His career, marked by audacious raids and a refusal to capitulate to colonial powers, established him as a feared figure.

Vane first emerged as a pirate in the aftermath of the War of Spanish Succession, a period that left many sailors unemployed and turned to piracy for survival. He was active in the Bahamas during the early 1710s, operating out of Nassau, which had become a pirate stronghold known as the "Republic of Pirates." Under Vane's command, his crew targeted merchant ships in the Caribbean, preying on the lucrative trade routes that connected Europe, Africa, and the Americas.

Vane was notorious for his brutality, often resorting to violence and intimidation to extract riches from his victims. One of his most infamous acts occurred when he captured a French vessel and burned it, along with its crew, as a message to others who might resist him. Such actions cemented his reputation as a ruthless pirate and struck fear into the hearts of his adversaries. However, this brutality was not without purpose; it was part of a broader strategy of psychological warfare that allowed Vane to achieve his goals with minimal resistance.

In 1718, the British government, determined to suppress piracy, offered a royal pardon to pirates willing to abandon their ways and return to lawful employment. Many prominent pirates, including Benjamin Hornigold and even the infamous Blackbeard, accepted the pardon, seeing it as an opportunity to escape the dangers of their trade. Charles Vane, however, refused. His rejection of the pardon was a bold declaration of his commitment to the pirate life and his disdain for authority, earning him the moniker "The Rebel Pirate."

Vane's defiance reached its peak when he encountered a fleet led by Woodes Rogers, the newly appointed Governor of the Bahamas, who was tasked with restoring order to Nassau. Rather than surrender, Vane attacked one of Rogers's ships and escaped with his crew. This act of open rebellion made him a symbol of resistance among those who still clung to the pirate way of life. However, it also made him a target of intensified efforts by colonial authorities to capture or kill him.

As a captain, Vane was known for his reckless bravery but also for his volatile temperament. His leadership was often called into question, particularly after a series of setbacks. In one notable incident, Vane encountered a powerful French warship and chose to flee rather than engage, prioritizing the safety of his crew over a potential victory. This decision angered his men, who accused him of cowardice and mutinied against him. Vane was deposed and replaced as captain by Calico Jack Rackham, who would later achieve his own notoriety in pirate history.

After his deposition, Vane continued his piratical activities with a smaller crew, but his fortunes steadily declined. His once-formidable reputation was diminished by his reduced resources and growing isolation. In 1719, his ship was wrecked on an uninhabited island in the Bay of Honduras during a storm. Stranded, Vane was eventually recognized and captured by the crew of a passing ship.

Vane was taken to Jamaica, where he was tried and convicted of piracy. Despite his claims that he had been coerced into piracy, the court showed no leniency. On March 29, 1721, Charles Vane was hanged in Port Royal.

Samuel Bellamy "Black Sam"

Samuel Bellamy was born in 1689 in Devon, England, to a poor family. From a young age, he was drawn to the sea, beginning his maritime career as a sailor. Like many of his contemporaries, he sought opportunities in the New World, traveling to Cape Cod, Massachusetts, around 1715. There, he reportedly fell in love with a young woman named Maria Hallett. However, Maria's family disapproved of the match due to Bellamy's lack of wealth and prospects. Determined to improve his fortunes, Bellamy set out to find his fortune, a decision that would ultimately lead him into piracy.

Bellamy's piratical career began in the aftermath of the wreck of the Spanish treasure fleet off the coast of Florida in 1715. He joined a group of treasure hunters searching for the vast wealth lost in the disaster. It was during this period that Bellamy met Paulsgrave Williams, who would become his trusted friend and partner in piracy. When their treasure-hunting efforts proved fruitless, Bellamy and Williams turned to piracy, seeking riches on the high seas rather than through legitimate means.

Bellamy quickly established himself as a bold and effective pirate captain. In 1716, he seized the Sultana, a ship that became his flagship and the foundation of his fleet. Known for his democratic leadership style, Bellamy treated his crew with respect and ensured that plunder was distributed fairly. This approach earned him the loyalty of his men and distinguished him from many other pirate captains of the time.

Bellamy's most famous capture came in 1717 when he seized the Whydah Gally, a heavily armed and richly laden slave ship. The Whydah carried gold, silver, ivory, and other valuables, making it one of the most lucrative prizes of the Golden Age of Piracy. Bellamy refitted the Whydah as his new flagship, transforming it into a symbol of his success and ambition. With the Whydah at the head of his fleet, Bellamy continued his campaign of piracy, targeting merchant ships along the eastern seaboard of North America and in the Caribbean.

Despite his success, Bellamy's career was short-lived. In April 1717, as the Whydah and its fleet sailed northward along the New England coast, they encountered a powerful storm near Cape Cod. The Whydah, heavily laden with plunder, was unable to withstand the gale. It sank, taking Bellamy and most of his crew with it. Only a handful of men survived, and the loss of the Whydah marked the tragic end of Bellamy's meteoric rise as a pirate captain.

In the centuries following his demise, his story has been romanticized, earning him the nickname "Black Sam" for his refusal to wear the powdered wigs of the time, favoring his natural black hair tied back instead. He became known as the "Robin Hood of the Sea," a moniker inspired by his reputation for generosity and fairness. Stories of Bellamy depict him as a man who stole from the rich and shared his spoils with his crew, embodying the idealized image of the noble pirate. The wreck of the Whydah was rediscovered in 1984 by underwater explorer Barry Clifford, and it remains the only verified pirate shipwreck ever recovered.

Stede Bonnet, "The Failed Pirate"

You don't have to be a Great Pirate to be famous. You can be a Great Loser - that works too. Unlike most pirates, who came from humble or troubled backgrounds, Bonnet was a wealthy landowner with no apparent maritime experience before embarking on a life of piracy. Born in 1688 to a prosperous family on the island of Barbados, Stede Bonnet inherited a large estate and significant wealth after the death of his parents. He lived a life of privilege, marrying Mary Allamby and settling into the role of a plantation owner. By all accounts, Bonnet's early life followed the conventional path expected of a man of his status. However, in 1717, he made a decision that shocked his contemporaries: he abandoned his comfortable life to become a pirate.

The reasons for Bonnet's dramatic shift remain unclear. Some historians speculate that he was driven by a midlife crisis or dissatisfaction with his domestic life. Others suggest he was inspired by romantic notions of adventure and freedom. Whatever his motivations, Bonnet's entry into piracy was unconventional. Unlike most pirates, who rose through the ranks of ship crews, Bonnet financed his own venture, commissioning the construction of a sloop he named Revenge. He hired a crew, paid them wages rather than sharing plunder, and set sail despite having no prior seafaring experience.

Bonnet's early attempts at piracy were lackluster. While he managed to capture a few merchant ships along the American coast, his lack of naval expertise and leadership skills quickly became apparent. His crew, frustrated with his incompetence, often ignored his orders. Bonnet also suffered injuries in a skirmish with a Spanish warship, further undermining his authority. Despite these setbacks, he persisted, determined to make a name for himself as a pirate.

In 1717, Bonnet encountered Edward Teach, better known as Blackbeard, one of the most notorious pirates of the era. The meeting would prove pivotal in Bonnet's career. Recognizing Bonnet's ineptitude, Blackbeard took command of the Revenge, relegating Bonnet to the status of a figurehead. Bonnet remained aboard as a guest, effectively sidelined while Blackbeard used the ship in his own piratical exploits. The partnership was short-lived, and Blackbeard eventually marooned Bonnet and his crew, further humiliating the would-be pirate.

Bonnet managed to regain control of the Revenge and continued his piratical activities, but his misfortunes persisted. In 1718, he accepted a royal pardon in an attempt to escape his precarious situation. Under the alias "Captain Thomas" and claiming to be a privateer, he resumed piracy shortly thereafter, betraying the terms of the pardon. His actions brought him to the attention of colonial authorities, who were determined to crack down on piracy in the region.

Bonnet's downfall came later that year when his ship was captured by Colonel William Rhett near the Cape Fear River in North Carolina. Taken to Charleston, South Carolina, Bonnet was tried for piracy. Despite his attempts to defend himself, including claims of being coerced into piracy, he was found guilty and sentenced to death. On December 10, 1718, Stede Bonnet was hanged, bringing his brief and calamitous career to an end.

Chapter 6: Pirate Myths and Mysteries

Buried Treasure Legends

The idea of buried pirate treasure has captivated imaginations for centuries, conjuring images of secret maps marked with an "X," chests brimming with gold coins and jewels, and daring hunts for hidden fortunes. These legends have been fueled by literature, folklore, and popular culture, creating a romanticized image of pirates carefully stashing their loot in remote locations to safeguard it from rivals and authorities. However, the reality behind these stories is far more complex and, in many cases, far less glamorous.

The concept of buried treasure as it exists in popular lore has little basis in historical fact. While pirates undoubtedly stole vast amounts of wealth, they rarely buried it. The nature of piracy itself—fast raids, immediate profit, and fleeting security—left little room for the long-term planning required to bury treasure. Pirates typically spent their plunder quickly, indulging in food, drink, gambling, and other pleasures in port towns like Nassau, Tortuga, or Port Royal. The life of a pirate was perilous and often short, making it unlikely that they would hide their riches for future use when survival in the present was uncertain.

Some pirates, however, may have hidden valuables temporarily for practical reasons. During raids, they might have buried or concealed treasure to prevent its capture by pursuing naval forces or rival pirates. These caches were intended to be retrieved soon after, not left behind for posterity. In such cases, the treasure was typically recovered successfully, leaving no lasting legacy of hidden hoards.

One of the most enduring myths of buried treasure involves Captain William Kidd, a privateer-turned-pirate whose name is synonymous with the idea of hidden loot. According to legend, Kidd buried a portion of his plunder on Gardiners Island off the coast of New York before his capture in 1699. Some of this treasure was indeed recovered and used as evidence against him during his trial in England, but the amount was relatively small. Despite this, tales of Kidd's buried treasure have persisted, inspiring countless treasure hunters to search for riches he may have hidden elsewhere. To date, no significant treasure linked to Kidd has been found.

Another source of buried treasure lore comes from literary works, particularly Robert Louis Stevenson's 1883 novel Treasure Island. The story of Long John Silver and a map leading to a hidden pirate hoard popularized the idea of treasure maps marked with an "X" to denote the spot where the riches were buried. While Treasure Island was a work of fiction, it drew on existing pirate myths and solidified the trope in popular culture. Subsequent books, films, and media built upon this imagery, embedding it deeply in the public imagination.

Despite the lack of historical evidence, buried treasure legends continue to fascinate, partly because they tap into universal themes of mystery, adventure, and the possibility of unearthing forgotten wealth. They also reflect the real and dramatic history of piracy, which was marked by vast fortunes won and lost, betrayal, and the fleeting nature of power and riches.

In some cases, treasure hunting has yielded remarkable discoveries, though they are rarely connected to legendary pirate hoards. Shipwrecks, rather than buried treasure, have been the most significant sources of recovered pirate wealth. The wreck of the Whydah Gally, Samuel Bellamy's flagship, was discovered in 1984 off the coast of Cape Cod and has yielded thousands of artifacts, including gold coins, jewelry, and weapons. Similarly, the Spanish treasure fleet of 1715, which sank off the coast of Florida, has been a rich source of recovered gold and silver, though these were not pirate treasures.

The Legend of the Flying Dutchman

The legend of the Flying Dutchman is one of the most enduring maritime myths, capturing imaginations for centuries with its tale of a ghost ship doomed to wander the seas for eternity. The origins of the legend are unclear, but it likely emerged in the 17th century during the height of Dutch maritime exploration and trade. The Flying Dutchman is often described as a large, menacing ship with tattered sails, glowing in an eerie light as it navigates treacherous waters. Its appearance, particularly during storms or fog, was considered an ill omen, foretelling disaster or death for those who encountered it.

The most common version of the legend tells of a Dutch captain, sometimes identified as Hendrik van der Decken, who was determined to complete his voyage despite a raging storm near the Cape of Good Hope. Defying the pleas of his crew and the natural limits of the sea, the captain swore an oath to round the cape, no matter the cost. His hubris, often depicted as a defiance of divine or natural laws, invoked a curse that condemned him and his ship to sail the oceans forever. In some versions of the tale, the curse is tied to the captain's blasphemous behavior or a pact with the devil.

Over time, sightings of the Flying Dutchman were reported by sailors navigating the unpredictable waters of the Cape of Good Hope, a notoriously dangerous passage. These accounts, often accompanied by descriptions of glowing lights or ghostly figures aboard the ship, added to the mythos. The ship was said to vanish as mysteriously as it appeared, leaving an air of dread in its wake.

One of the most famous alleged sightings occurred in 1881 when the future King George V of England, then a midshipman, reported seeing the Flying Dutchman while aboard the HMS Bacchante. According to the ship's log, a glowing red ship was seen on the horizon, only to disappear moments later. Such accounts, though rare, lent credibility to the legend and reinforced its status as a cautionary tale for sailors.

The Flying Dutchman legend has inspired countless adaptations in literature, opera, and film. In 1843, German composer Richard Wagner premiered his opera Der fliegende Holländer (The Flying Dutchman), which reimagined the tale as a story of redemption and eternal love. The opera's haunting music and dramatic themes helped solidify the ship's place in Western cultural imagination.

In modern times, the Flying Dutchman has continued to capture the public's fascination, appearing in novels, movies, and television shows. Its portrayal in the Pirates of the Caribbean film series, where it serves as a cursed ship commanded by Davy Jones, is one of the most recognizable modern interpretations. The ship's eerie presence and supernatural qualities remain central to its mystique.

For sailors of earlier centuries, the legend reflected the dangers and uncertainties of life at sea, where storms, shipwrecks, and death were constant threats. The story also speaks to deeper fears of isolation and the unknown, as well as the human tendency to create meaning from unexplained phenomena.

The Kraken

This mythical sea monster, described as a massive, tentacled beast capable of dragging entire ships and their crews to the ocean floor, has captivated imaginations for centuries. While rooted in ancient maritime folklore, the Kraken's legend grew alongside the golden age of piracy, becoming an emblem of the ocean's untamed and enigmatic power.

The Kraken legend originates in Scandinavian folklore, where it was first described as an enormous creature dwelling in the deep waters of the North Atlantic. Early accounts depicted the Kraken as so large that it resembled an island when seen from afar. Sailors and fishermen spoke of the beast creating powerful whirlpools as it submerged, capable of capsizing ships and pulling them into the abyss. For pirates navigating the treacherous waters near Greenland, Iceland, and Norway, such stories added a layer of fear to an already perilous existence.

The fearsome image of the Kraken was shaped by both superstition and the natural dangers of the sea. Sudden, unexplained shipwrecks, violent storms, and disappearing vessels were attributed to the creature, offering sailors an explanation for events beyond their control. For pirates, who often operated in uncharted waters and faced constant risks, the Kraken symbolized the unpredictability of their world and the idea that even the most skilled seafarers could fall victim to nature's wrath.

One of the earliest detailed accounts of the Kraken came from Erik Pontoppidan, a Danish-Norwegian bishop and naturalist, in his 1752 book The Natural History of Norway. Pontoppidan described the Kraken as a colossal beast capable of creating whirlpools that threatened entire fleets. Although his account blended folklore with speculation, it solidified the Kraken's place in European maritime legend and spread its story beyond Scandinavia.

The legend of the Kraken may have been inspired by sightings of real sea creatures, particularly the giant squid (Architeuthis dux), which can grow up to 50 feet in length. For sailors, encountering parts of these creatures—such as washed-up tentacles or massive eyes—must have been both awe-inspiring and terrifying. Lacking the scientific knowledge to explain such discoveries, they wove them into myths, and the Kraken became a larger-than-life representation of these mysterious animals.

Pirates were particularly susceptible to such legends, given the dangers they faced at sea and their reliance on oral storytelling to pass the time during long voyages. Stories of the Kraken likely circulated widely among pirate crews, adding to the mystique of the open ocean and reinforcing the idea that certain parts of the sea were cursed or inhabited by monstrous beings. These tales served as both entertainment and warnings, reminding pirates of the dangers lurking in the depths.

As the Kraken legend spread, it found a place in literature and art, further embedding itself in maritime culture. The Kraken became a symbol of the ocean's vastness and the limits of human control. Romantic poets like Alfred Lord Tennyson gave the creature a mythical grandeur in works such as "The Kraken," portraying it as an ancient, slumbering force. This poetic depiction reflected the awe and mystery associated with the deep sea, resonating with readers and reinforcing the Kraken's legendary status.

In the context of pirate myths, the Kraken often took on a symbolic role as the ultimate test of courage and survival. Stories of pirates battling or outwitting the Kraken became staples of maritime lore, highlighting the daring and resourcefulness required to navigate the seas.

The Disappearance of Henry Avery

Avery was born around 1659 in England, likely in the small village of Newton Ferrers near Plymouth. Little is known about his early life, but he worked as a sailor in the Royal Navy and aboard merchant vessels before turning to piracy. His career as a pirate began in 1694 when he led a mutiny aboard the Charles II, a privateer ship. Renaming the vessel Fancy, Avery and his crew embarked on a career of piracy that would make him legendary.

Avery's most famous exploit occurred in 1695 when he and his crew captured the Ganj-i-Sawai, a massive treasure ship belonging to the Mughal Empire. The Ganj-i-Sawai was returning from Mecca with pilgrims and was heavily laden with gold, silver, and jewels. Despite being well-armed and accompanied by an escort ship, the Ganj-i-Sawai fell to Avery after a fierce battle. The haul from this single raid was staggering, making Avery and his crew fabulously wealthy.

The raid, however, had far-reaching consequences. The Mughal Empire, outraged by the attack, demanded retribution from the British East India Company, threatening their trading privileges in India. This political pressure led to one of the first global manhunts for a pirate, with Avery and his crew becoming the targets of both British and Mughal authorities.

Despite the intense search, Avery managed to evade capture, but his fate after the raid remains one of piracy's great mysteries. Historical records suggest that Avery and his crew sailed to the Bahamas, where they likely bribed local officials in exchange for safe passage. Some of his crew dispersed, settling in various colonies or returning to England, while others were arrested and executed. Avery himself disappeared from public records, leaving behind only fragments of rumor and speculation.

One theory suggests that Avery returned to England, hoping to live quietly under an assumed name. Some accounts claim he was cheated out of his fortune by merchants who promised to launder his wealth in exchange for a share, leaving him penniless and destitute. Other stories suggest he may have died in poverty, unable to enjoy the riches he had risked everything to obtain.

Another theory posits that Avery fled to a remote location, perhaps an uninhabited island or an obscure colony, where he lived out the rest of his days in secrecy. The possibility of Avery successfully escaping with his vast treasure has fueled legends of hidden pirate hoards, with treasure hunters and historians alike speculating about the whereabouts of his ill-gotten gains.

Avery's disappearance and the lack of concrete evidence about his fate have only added to his mystique. Unlike many pirates who met violent ends or were captured and executed, Avery's ability to vanish elevated him to near-mythical status. His story became a source of fascination for writers and chroniclers of the time, with early accounts embellishing his exploits and framing him as a cunning and elusive figure.

The Mystery of Blackbeard's Ghost

Blackbeard's death is among the most legendary events in pirate history. After years of terrorizing the seas, he was cornered off the coast of Ocracoke Island, North Carolina, by Lieutenant Robert Maynard of the British Royal Navy. In a fierce battle, Blackbeard reportedly sustained over 20 wounds, including five gunshots, before finally succumbing. His head was severed and displayed on the bowsprit of Maynard's ship as a warning to other pirates. His body, according to legend, was thrown overboard. Sailors claimed that his headless corpse swam around the ship three times before sinking—a macabre detail that hinted at Blackbeard's indomitable spirit even in death.

This dramatic end laid the groundwork for tales of Blackbeard's ghost. One of the most persistent legends centers on Teach's Hole, the stretch of water near Ocracoke Island where Blackbeard met his end. Locals and visitors have reported seeing mysterious lights hovering over the water at night, believed to be the ghostly lantern of Blackbeard searching for his severed head. These "ghost lights," often called St. Elmo's fire or similar atmospheric phenomena, are interpreted as signs of Blackbeard's restless spirit.

The legend of Blackbeard's ghost is further fueled by the superstition surrounding his hidden treasure. Blackbeard was rumored to have buried vast amounts of gold and valuables in secret locations, claiming that only he and the devil knew their whereabouts. While no definitive treasure linked to Blackbeard has ever been found, the idea of untold riches lying in wait has inspired countless treasure hunts and added to the mystique of his ghost.

Another locale tied to Blackbeard's ghost is Bath, North Carolina, where he is said to have spent time between voyages. Stories persist of a spectral figure, dressed in Blackbeard's characteristic attire, wandering the streets or appearing near his supposed former residence. These sightings are often accompanied by an inexplicable chill or the sound of heavy footsteps, reinforcing the belief that the pirate's spirit has not fully departed.

The Role of Storytellers

The transformation of pirates from historical figures into cultural icons owes much to the work of storytellers—writers, chroniclers, and entertainers—who have shaped the public's understanding of piracy. These narratives, blending fact and fiction, have ensured that pirates remain enduring symbols of adventure, rebellion, and mystery.

The origins of pirate folklore can be traced to the sailors and coastal communities that encountered pirates firsthand. During the Golden Age of Piracy in the 17th and early 18th centuries, tales of pirate raids, ship battles, and buried treasure were shared orally, often embellished for dramatic effect. Sailors returning from voyages would recount harrowing encounters with infamous pirates like Blackbeard, Bartholomew Roberts, and Anne Bonny, feeding the public's fascination with these enigmatic figures. These stories, passed from port to port, formed the foundation of pirate folklore, capturing both the fear and allure of the pirate life.

Pirates themselves contributed to their own mythos. Many cultivated fearsome reputations deliberately, using theatrical displays and exaggerated tales to intimidate their enemies. The written word played a crucial role in cementing piracy's place in popular imagination. In 1724, the publication of A General History of the Robberies and Murders of the Most Notorious Pyrates by Captain Charles Johnson marked a turning point. This book, a sensationalized account of pirate lives and exploits, introduced readers to figures like Blackbeard, Mary Read, and Captain Kidd. While its authorship remains disputed—some suggest it was Daniel Defoe—A General History combined factual events with dramatic embellishments, creating vivid narratives that captivated audiences and shaped the modern perception of pirates.

Literature further elevated pirates into the realm of legend. In 1883, Robert Louis Stevenson's Treasure Island revolutionized the genre with its portrayal of Long John Silver and his crew. Stevenson's novel introduced iconic elements of pirate lore, including treasure maps marked with an "X," parrots perched on shoulders, and the archetype of the cunning yet charismatic pirate. These elements, though largely fictional, became staples of pirate imagery and continue to influence how pirates are depicted in popular culture.

Other writers, such as J.M. Barrie with Peter Pan, further romanticized piracy, presenting it as a fantastical and adventurous alternative to the constraints of ordinary life. Pirates in these stories were often portrayed as both villains and symbols of freedom, embodying the duality of piracy as a dangerous yet alluring way of life.

Folklore and literature were not the only mediums that shaped the pirate mythos. Ballads, stage plays, and later, films brought pirate stories to new audiences. Songs like "The Ballad of Captain Kidd" recounted the exploits and fate of the infamous pirate, blending moral lessons with entertainment. Theater productions often dramatized pirate raids and sea battles, emphasizing their swashbuckling appeal.

In the 20th and 21st centuries, pirates became fixtures of popular culture through film and television. Early Hollywood films like Captain Blood (1935) and The Sea Hawk (1940) romanticized piracy, presenting dashing heroes and thrilling adventures on the high seas. Storytellers have taken the raw material of piracy—its danger, drama, and mystery—and woven it into narratives that transcend time, making pirates a permanent fixture in global folklore and literature.

Chapter 7: The Consequences of Piracy

At its core, piracy was driven by the pursuit of profit. Pirates preyed on merchant ships transporting valuable commodities such as gold, silver, spices, sugar, and textiles. These goods were integral to the global economy, fueling the mercantile systems of European empires and their colonial enterprises. By intercepting these shipments, pirates directly disrupted the flow of wealth between colonies and their parent nations. This disruption was particularly acute in the Caribbean and along the Spanish Main, where Spanish treasure fleets transported enormous quantities of gold and silver from the Americas to Europe.

Piracy undermined the profitability of colonial trade by increasing the costs of shipping. Merchants and governments were forced to invest heavily in armed escorts, fortified ports, and naval patrols to protect their vessels and cargoes. Insurance premiums for shipping skyrocketed in regions plagued by piracy, further inflating the costs of trade. These expenses often strained colonial economies and reduced the profits of trading companies, leading to calls for more aggressive anti-piracy measures.

The pirate economy also had a paradoxical effect on local markets and coastal communities. While pirates disrupted trade routes, they also stimulated commerce in certain areas by acting as alternative suppliers of goods. Pirates frequently sold stolen goods at significantly reduced prices in pirate havens such as Nassau in the Bahamas, Port Royal in Jamaica, and Tortuga off the coast of Hispaniola. These black markets allowed local merchants and settlers to acquire goods they might otherwise have been unable to afford or access due to colonial monopolies and restrictive trade practices.

Moreover, pirates themselves contributed to the economies of the regions where they operated. They spent their plunder lavishly on food, drink, clothing, and entertainment, injecting wealth into local communities. Pirate ports became vibrant, though lawless, centers of commerce, attracting a mix of sailors, traders, and opportunists. In some cases, colonial officials and merchants colluded with pirates, turning a blind eye to their activities in exchange for a share of the profits. This complicity blurred the lines between legal and illegal trade, revealing the extent to which piracy was integrated into the broader economic system.

The global reach of piracy also exposed the vulnerabilities of imperial trade networks. European powers such as Spain, England, France, and the Netherlands relied heavily on maritime commerce to sustain their colonial empires and fund their wars. The success of pirates in attacking these networks highlighted the limitations of naval power and the challenges of protecting far-flung colonies. This realization prompted nations to invest in larger and more sophisticated navies, leading to advancements in ship design, navigation, and maritime warfare.

The impact of piracy on global trade was not entirely negative. By challenging monopolies and disrupting traditional trade routes, pirates inadvertently spurred innovation and adaptation in the maritime industry. Merchants developed new strategies to evade pirate attacks, such as altering shipping schedules, using faster ships, and diversifying trade routes. Governments also introduced legal and administrative reforms, including the establishment of admiralty courts and the use of privateers—state-sanctioned pirates—to combat piracy.

The Slave Trade

The transatlantic slave trade was one of the most significant and harrowing aspects of global commerce during the 17th and 18th centuries, and pirates played a complex role in its operations. While piracy is often romanticized as a rebellion against authority, pirates were deeply entwined with the systems of exploitation they operated within. Some pirates actively disrupted the slave trade by attacking ships and diverting profits, while others exploited the trade for their own gain, capturing and selling enslaved people as commodities.

The transatlantic slave trade was central to the economies of European colonial powers. Ships carried millions of enslaved Africans to the Americas, where they were forced to work on plantations producing sugar, tobacco, cotton, and other lucrative commodities. These goods were then shipped to Europe, completing a triangular trade that generated immense wealth for colonial empires. Slave ships, heavily laden with human cargo, were prime targets for pirates due to the significant profits they represented.

Pirates often attacked slave ships during their transatlantic journeys, capturing both the ships and their human cargo. These attacks disrupted the trade by reducing the supply of enslaved people to colonial markets, causing temporary shortages and financial losses for slave traders. However, the motives of pirates were rarely altruistic. They saw slave ships as opportunities for plunder and profit. Enslaved individuals, considered valuable commodities, could be sold at pirate havens or other ports where laws were lax or enforcement was weak.

In some cases, pirates freed the enslaved individuals they captured, integrating them into their crews. Pirate ships were known for their relatively egalitarian practices compared to the rigid hierarchies of the colonial world, and enslaved people who joined pirate crews often found a degree of freedom unavailable elsewhere. These individuals, once aboard pirate ships, were treated as equals and shared in the risks and rewards of piracy. Notable examples include Black Caesar, an African who became a prominent pirate operating in the Caribbean after escaping enslavement.

Despite these instances of liberation, many pirates actively participated in the slave trade, exploiting it for personal gain. Pirates who captured slave ships often resold their human cargo to plantation owners or middlemen at reduced prices. This practice allowed pirates to profit from the trade while undercutting the official market, further destabilizing colonial economies. Some pirate havens, such as Nassau in the Bahamas and Port Royal in Jamaica, became hubs for this illicit trade, blending piracy with the broader system of colonial exploitation.

While pirates operated outside the bounds of the law, their actions were often facilitated by the same systems that sustained colonial empires. Corrupt officials, merchants, and plantation owners frequently colluded with pirates, turning a blind eye to their activities or actively supporting them in exchange for access to cheap labor and goods.

Pirates' impact on the slave trade was not uniform and varied depending on the region and circumstances. In some areas, their attacks disrupted the trade and exposed its vulnerabilities, forcing colonial powers to invest in stronger defenses and naval patrols. In others, pirates acted as opportunistic participants, exploiting the trade for their own benefit while perpetuating the system of human exploitation.

Insurance and Security Measures

Piracy represented a substantial financial risk to merchants, who often transported valuable cargoes such as gold, silver, spices, textiles, and sugar across vast oceans. These threats compelled merchants, governments, and insurers to adapt, leading to innovations that would shape maritime practices for generations. A successful pirate attack could result in the total loss of a ship and its cargo, devastating a merchant's livelihood and disrupting trade networks. To mitigate these risks, the maritime insurance industry became an essential part of global trade. Insurers provided merchants with financial protection against piracy, covering the value of both the ship and its cargo in exchange for premiums.

The rise in piracy led to a corresponding increase in insurance premiums, particularly for voyages through high-risk areas like the Caribbean, the Indian Ocean, and the Spanish Main. These elevated costs reflected the frequency and severity of pirate attacks, and they often made shipping significantly more expensive. Some merchants passed these costs on to consumers, driving up the prices of imported goods. In extreme cases, the threat of piracy deterred merchants from operating in certain regions altogether, disrupting trade routes and limiting economic growth.

To address these challenges, insurers developed more sophisticated methods of assessing and pricing risk. Detailed records of pirate activity were maintained, allowing insurers to identify patterns and adjust premiums accordingly. This practice not only helped insurers manage their exposure to losses but also provided valuable intelligence for merchants and shipowners, who could use the information to plan safer routes and schedules.

In addition to relying on insurance, merchants and governments implemented a variety of security measures to protect their ships from pirate attacks. Convoys became a common strategy, with groups of merchant ships sailing together under the protection of armed escorts. These convoys, often organized by naval forces, provided a degree of safety in numbers and reduced the likelihood of individual ships being targeted by pirates. However, the reliance on convoys also introduced delays and logistical challenges, as ships had to coordinate their departures and maintain formation during their voyages.

Ship design also evolved in response to the threat of piracy. Merchant vessels were increasingly equipped with defensive features such as reinforced hulls, swivel guns, and higher decks to deter boarding attempts. Some ships were built for speed, allowing them to outrun pirate vessels, while others were armed to resist attacks. These adaptations reflected the growing need for merchants to balance the trade-off between security and operational efficiency.

Naval patrols and anti-piracy campaigns were another critical component of maritime security during this period. Governments invested heavily in expanding their navies, deploying warships to patrol pirate-infested waters and protect vital trade routes. These patrols not only provided direct protection to merchant ships but also served as a deterrent, forcing pirates to operate in more remote and less profitable areas. The establishment of naval bases in strategic locations further enhanced the ability of colonial powers to respond to pirate activity.

The introduction of privateers—state-sanctioned pirates—was another measure aimed at combating piracy. Privateers were authorized to attack enemy ships during times of war, and their activities often targeted pirate vessels as well. Despite these efforts, piracy remained a persistent threat for much of the Golden Age, reflecting the challenges of enforcing security across vast and often poorly regulated oceans.

Chapter 8: The Decline of the Golden Age

Anti-Piracy Legislation

The threat of piracy prompted governments around the world to develop and enforce anti-piracy legislation aimed at protecting maritime trade and asserting control over the seas. These laws were not merely reactive measures; they reflected the growing recognition of piracy as a serious threat to economic stability, international relations, and the authority of emerging global powers. By criminalizing piracy, streamlining prosecution, and deploying legal frameworks to pursue offenders, these laws sought to suppress piracy and restore order to the oceans.

One of the earliest and most significant legal foundations for combating piracy was the principle of universal jurisdiction. Piracy, defined as robbery or criminal violence on the high seas, was considered hostis humani generis, or an "enemy of all mankind." This designation allowed any nation, regardless of where the crime occurred, to capture and prosecute pirates. This international approach to piracy was crucial in addressing a crime that transcended national boundaries and operated in the lawless expanses of the open sea.

The English government played a leading role in developing anti-piracy legislation, reflecting the centrality of maritime trade to its economy. In 1536, England enacted the first comprehensive anti-piracy law under the reign of King Henry VIII. This law allowed pirates to be tried in admiralty courts, bypassing traditional jury trials to expedite prosecution. These courts, staffed by naval officers and legal experts, were designed to handle maritime cases efficiently, reducing the procedural delays that often hindered justice on land.

The Piracy Act of 1698 was another landmark in anti-piracy legislation. Passed during a period of heightened pirate activity in the Caribbean and Atlantic, the act provided clearer definitions of piracy and established harsher penalties, including death. It also expanded the jurisdiction of admiralty courts, enabling them to prosecute pirates captured anywhere in the world. The law was accompanied by efforts to incentivize the capture of pirates, including financial rewards for naval officers and private citizens who apprehended them.

The early 18th century saw further refinements in anti-piracy laws, driven by the increasing severity of pirate attacks and their impact on global trade. The Piracy Act of 1717 introduced measures to encourage pirates to surrender by offering royal pardons to those who renounced piracy and cooperated with authorities. This act, known as the "Act for the Suppression of Piracy," was part of a broader strategy to weaken pirate networks by dividing loyalties and reducing their numbers. The pardons, while controversial, were effective in persuading many pirates to abandon their trade, including prominent figures like Benjamin Hornigold.

International cooperation was another key component of anti-piracy efforts. Treaties between European powers facilitated joint naval patrols and the extradition of pirates. For example, agreements between Britain, Spain, and Portugal allowed for shared intelligence and mutual enforcement of anti-piracy laws. These collaborations reflected the shared interest of colonial powers in suppressing piracy to protect their trade routes and colonial holdings.

Despite these legal measures, enforcing anti-piracy laws was a significant challenge. Pirates operated in remote regions, often with the complicity of local officials or communities who benefited from their activities. Pirate havens like Nassau in the Bahamas and Tortuga in the Caribbean provided safe harbors where pirates could refit their ships, sell stolen goods, and evade capture. To address this, colonial administrations were restructured, and governors with strong naval backgrounds, such as Woodes Rogers in the Bahamas, were appointed to enforce anti-piracy laws and restore order.

Woodes Rogers and Pirate Hunters

The threat posed by pirates prompted colonial powers to deploy specialized pirate hunters, whose missions were to capture or eliminate pirates and restore order to the seas. Among the most notable figures in this effort was Woodes

Rogers, a former privateer turned royal governor, whose campaigns against piracy in the Bahamas became a defining example of how naval and administrative strategies were used to suppress the pirate menace. Rogers's tenure in the Caribbean marked a turning point in the fight against piracy and showcased the effectiveness of combining military force with governance and diplomacy.

Woodes Rogers, born in 1679 in England, was a privateer with extensive maritime experience. He earned fame during an earlier circumnavigation of the globe (1708–1711) when he rescued castaway Alexander Selkirk, whose story inspired Daniel Defoe's Robinson Crusoe. Rogers's experience as a privateer prepared him for the complexities of navigating the lawless waters of the Caribbean, where pirates like Blackbeard, Charles Vane, and Calico Jack Rackham operated with relative impunity.

By the early 18th century, the Bahamas, particularly Nassau, had become a notorious pirate haven. The weak colonial administration and the region's proximity to major trade routes allowed pirates to thrive. Nassau, referred to as the "Republic of Pirates," was a hotbed of lawlessness, where pirate crews operated openly, refitting their ships and trading stolen goods. The British government, recognizing the strategic importance of the Bahamas and the economic damage caused by piracy, decided to take decisive action.

In 1718, Woodes Rogers was appointed the first royal governor of the Bahamas with a dual mandate: to eradicate piracy and establish effective colonial governance. Upon his arrival in Nassau, Rogers faced an uphill battle. The town was under de facto pirate control, and the infrastructure and defenses were in a state of disrepair. Pirates such as Charles Vane openly resisted Rogers's authority, viewing his arrival as a direct threat to their autonomy.

Rogers employed a combination of military force, diplomacy, and legal measures to achieve his objectives. His most immediate tool was the royal pardon, issued by King George I, which offered clemency to pirates who surrendered and renounced their criminal activities. This tactic divided pirate ranks, as some, like Benjamin Hornigold, accepted the pardon and transitioned into legitimate roles, while others, like Vane, continued their defiance.

Rogers's use of the pardon was accompanied by a show of military strength. He brought with him a small fleet of warships and a contingent of soldiers to enforce the king's authority. These forces were instrumental in repelling pirate resistance and reestablishing control over Nassau. Charles Vane, one of the most prominent holdouts, fled Nassau after a failed attempt to burn Rogers's ships, leaving the town vulnerable to Rogers's efforts to rebuild and fortify it.

Rogers also worked to restore order through governance. He established a functioning administration, repaired Nassau's defenses, and encouraged trade to revitalize the local economy. His efforts to transform Nassau from a pirate stronghold into a legitimate colony were met with mixed success, as the challenges of corruption, limited resources, and lingering pirate influence persisted.

However, his leadership laid the groundwork for the eventual stabilization of the Bahamas.

The deployment of pirate hunters like Rogers marked a shift in the approach to combating piracy. Rather than relying solely on reactive naval patrols, colonial powers began to focus on proactive strategies that combined military action with administrative reform. Rogers's tenure demonstrated the importance of addressing the root causes of piracy, such as weak governance and economic instability, rather than merely targeting individual pirates.

Rogers's success in suppressing piracy in the Bahamas contributed to the decline of the Golden Age of Piracy. His efforts, along with those of other pirate hunters and naval campaigns, made the Caribbean increasingly inhospitable to pirates.

The Decline of Safe Havens

Pirate strongholds were critical to the survival and success of pirates, offering secure locations to repair ships, resupply, and trade stolen goods. These havens thrived in regions where colonial governments were weak or absent, creating lawless enclaves that challenged imperial authority.

Nassau, located on New Providence Island in the Bahamas, was perhaps the most infamous of the pirate strongholds. By the early 18th century, it had become a de facto "Republic of Pirates," home to notorious figures such as Charles Vane, Blackbeard, Calico Jack Rackham, and Anne Bonny. Its strategic location near major trade routes and its natural harbor made Nassau an ideal base for pirate operations. The town lacked a functioning government, and its small, underfunded militia was unable to resist the influx of pirates who turned Nassau into a bustling hub of illicit activity.

Pirates in Nassau operated with impunity, trading plundered goods, recruiting crew members, and refitting their ships. The lack of oversight also allowed them to establish their own informal systems of governance. In many ways, Nassau embodied the pirate ideal of freedom, as it was a place where individuals could live outside the constraints of colonial hierarchies and pursue wealth on their own terms. However, this autonomy came at a cost, as Nassau's lawlessness posed a direct threat to the economic and political stability of the region.

The British government, alarmed by the impact of piracy on trade and colonial interests, made the suppression of pirate havens a priority. In 1718, King George I issued a royal proclamation offering pardons to pirates who surrendered and renounced their criminal activities. This strategy aimed to weaken pirate networks by encouraging defections and isolating the more defiant leaders. The proclamation was accompanied by the appointment of Woodes Rogers as the first royal governor of the Bahamas.

Rogers's arrival in Nassau in 1718 marked the beginning of the end for the pirate stronghold. Rogers implemented a series of reforms to transform Nassau from a pirate haven into a functioning colony. He fortified the town, rebuilt its defenses, and established a legal and administrative framework to enforce British authority. The presence of a permanent garrison and regular naval patrols deterred pirates from returning, while the integration of former pirates into colonial society helped to stabilize the region.

The fall of Nassau was part of a broader trend in the decline of pirate havens. Similar efforts were undertaken in other key locations, such as Port Royal in Jamaica, Tortuga off the coast of Hispaniola, and the island of Madagascar. These havens, once vital to the pirate economy, were systematically dismantled as colonial powers extended their reach and asserted control over maritime trade routes. The establishment of stronger naval patrols, fortified ports, and centralized governance reduced the opportunities for pirates to find refuge and resupply.

The loss of safe havens dealt a critical blow to piracy. Without secure bases, pirates faced increasing logistical challenges, from maintaining their ships to disposing of their plunder. They also became more vulnerable to capture, as they could no longer rely on the protection of sympathetic communities or corrupt officials.

Betrayals and Executions

The decline of the Golden Age of Piracy was marked by dramatic shifts in fortune for many of its most infamous figures. Betrayals, captures, and public executions played pivotal roles in turning the tide against pirates, demonstrating the increasing resolve of colonial powers to eradicate piracy and assert control over maritime trade. These events, often sensationalized and widely publicized, signaled a turning point in the fight against piracy, transforming former pirate heroes into cautionary tales and examples of justice.

One of the most significant factors leading to the downfall of pirates was betrayal, often by their own allies or associates. As colonial governments began offering pardons and rewards for information, the pirate community became fractured. Former comrades, faced with the prospect of execution or the promise of financial gain, turned against one another. Betrayals became common, eroding the trust and unity that had once allowed pirate crews to operate effectively.

The capture and execution of Charles Vane exemplify this shift. Vane, one of the most notorious and defiant pirates of his time, was known for his ruthless tactics and refusal to accept royal pardons. After being deposed by his own crew and cast adrift, Vane's fortunes dwindled. He was eventually recognized by an acquaintance and handed over to colonial authorities in Jamaica. Vane was tried, convicted, and hanged in 1721, his death serving as a stark warning to others who refused to abandon piracy.

Public executions played a crucial role in the campaign against pirates, serving as both punishment and spectacle. Executions were often carried out in highly visible locations, such as harbors or gallows along busy trade routes, to send a clear message to other pirates and the general public. The bodies of executed pirates were sometimes displayed in gibbets, their decaying remains serving as grim reminders of the consequences of defying colonial law.

These dramatic events were part of a broader strategy by colonial powers to shift public perception of piracy. While pirates had once been celebrated in some circles as rebellious figures or folk heroes, their betrayals and executions painted them as criminals who posed a threat to economic stability and governance. By publicizing these events, governments sought to delegitimize piracy and discourage others from joining its ranks.

How Diplomacy Undermined Piracy

Piracy often thrived during periods of war and conflict, when privateering—a form of state-sanctioned piracy—was a common strategy for weakening enemy nations. Privateers were granted letters of marque by their governments, authorizing them to attack and plunder enemy ships. While privateers operated within the bounds of legality, many blurred the line between privateering and outright piracy, attacking ships of neutral or allied nations and keeping the spoils for themselves. The chaotic environment of war made it difficult for governments to regulate these activities, allowing piracy to flourish in the shadows of legitimate maritime conflict.

The end of the War of the Spanish Succession in 1713 marked a significant turning point. The Treaty of Utrecht, which concluded the war, brought relative peace to Europe and reshaped colonial power dynamics. One of the treaty's key provisions was the reduction of privateering activities. With fewer opportunities to operate under the guise of privateering, many sailors who had depended on wartime commissions turned to outright piracy to sustain themselves. This post-war surge in piracy, particularly in the Caribbean and Atlantic, alarmed colonial powers and prompted coordinated efforts to suppress it.

Peace treaties like the Treaty of Utrecht also fostered greater cooperation between European nations in combating piracy. While these nations had previously tolerated or even supported piracy as a tool against their rivals, the treaties emphasized the importance of protecting trade and stabilizing colonial economies. Maritime commerce, a cornerstone of European wealth, was increasingly seen as a shared interest that required collective action to safeguard. This shift led to joint naval patrols, intelligence-sharing, and extradition agreements that made it more difficult for pirates to evade capture.

The end of hostilities also allowed colonial powers to redirect their naval resources toward anti-piracy campaigns. During times of war, navies were primarily focused on defending territories and engaging enemy fleets, leaving many trade routes vulnerable to pirate attacks. With the return of peace, these resources could be deployed to protect merchant shipping and dismantle pirate networks. The establishment of naval bases in strategic locations, such as Jamaica and the Bahamas, further enhanced the ability of European powers to enforce maritime security.

The collaboration between England and Spain illustrates this shift. Once bitter rivals, the two nations found common ground in addressing the pirate threat, particularly in the Caribbean, where piracy disrupted trade routes critical to both empires. This newfound cooperation allowed for joint operations against notorious pirate strongholds like Nassau, which was reclaimed by England under the leadership of Woodes Rogers. Similar agreements between France and England further limited the ability of pirates to exploit national rivalries for their benefit.

During times of war, pirates and privateers were often romanticized as daring adventurers or patriotic defenders of their nations. In the aftermath of peace treaties, however, governments sought to delegitimize piracy by emphasizing its criminal nature and the harm it caused to commerce and stability. This narrative shift, combined with the visible consequences of anti-piracy campaigns—such as the executions of captured pirates—diminished the appeal of piracy and discouraged potential recruits.

The End of Privateering

Privateering was formalized through the issuance of letters of marque, legal documents granting shipowners permission to attack vessels belonging to enemy nations. These letters specified the conditions under which privateers could operate, including the sharing of captured prizes with the government. For centuries, privateering was a mutually beneficial arrangement: governments gained auxiliary naval forces without incurring the costs of building and maintaining additional warships, while privateers reaped substantial profits from their captures.

Many privateers used their commissions as a cover for attacking neutral or allied ships, keeping the profits for themselves and undermining the legitimacy of their actions. Others continued raiding long after their letters of marque had expired, effectively transitioning into full-fledged piracy. The chaotic nature of maritime warfare made it difficult for governments to regulate privateers, leading to widespread abuses that tarnished the practice's reputation. Although privateering outlived the Caribbean pirates, the fight against it began in the early 1700s, just after the end of major regional conflicts. This dealt a severe blow to piracy in the Caribbean and hastened the end of the Golden Age.

The conclusion of major European conflicts, such as the War of the Spanish Succession (1701–1714) and the Napoleonic Wars (1803–1815), further exposed the flaws in privateering. During times of peace, privateers found themselves unemployed, and many turned to piracy to sustain their livelihoods. The transition from legal privateering to illegal piracy was not uncommon, as the skills and infrastructure required for both activities were virtually identical. This contributed to the surge in piracy that followed the end of these wars, creating significant challenges for governments seeking to maintain order on the seas.

The growing consensus among nations that privateering disrupted global trade and created long-term instability led to efforts to abolish the practice. The turning point came with the Declaration of Paris in 1856, a landmark international agreement signed by major European powers, including Britain, France, and Russia. The declaration, which emerged in the aftermath of the Crimean War, explicitly banned privateering, marking the first major step toward establishing a uniform code of conduct for naval warfare. The United States, though not a signatory, adhered to the principles of the declaration in practice, further reinforcing its impact.

The abolition of privateering reflected the changing nature of warfare and the rise of modern naval power. By the mid-19th century, advancements in shipbuilding, weaponry, and communication had made privateering less relevant as a military strategy. National navies became more centralized and professionalized, reducing the need to rely on private citizens to supplement maritime defense. The risks associated with privateering, including the potential for diplomatic conflicts and the erosion of international trust, outweighed its benefits in an era of increasingly interconnected global trade.

The British Navy's Supremacy

The Royal Navy's dominance was built on a combination of technological innovation, organizational discipline, and strategic deployment. British warships of the era, including heavily armed frigates and smaller, agile sloops-of-war, were designed to outmatch the speed and firepower of pirate vessels. Unlike pirate ships, which were often repurposed merchant or fishing vessels, Royal Navy ships were purpose-built for combat, featuring reinforced hulls, superior rigging, and advanced weaponry such as broadside cannons and swivel guns. These technological advantages gave the British Navy a decisive edge in naval engagements.

The navy's organizational structure also played a key role in its effectiveness. British warships were commanded by experienced officers and manned by professional sailors who underwent rigorous training. This level of discipline and coordination stood in stark contrast to pirate crews, which were often loosely organized and reliant on opportunistic tactics. The Royal Navy's ability to execute complex maneuvers and maintain formation during battle allowed it to overwhelm pirate fleets, even when outnumbered.

Beyond the Caribbean, the Royal Navy extended its anti-piracy campaigns to the Indian Ocean, where pirates like Henry Every and Thomas Tew had targeted lucrative trade routes connecting Europe, Africa, and Asia. British warships patrolled these waters, protecting merchant vessels and engaging pirate ships in decisive battles. The navy's presence in the region not only suppressed piracy but also reinforced Britain's dominance in global trade.

The capture and execution of notorious pirates further demonstrated the Royal Navy's effectiveness. Figures like Blackbeard, Bartholomew Roberts, and Calico Jack Rackham fell to naval campaigns, their deaths serving as both practical victories and symbolic warnings. In many cases, the navy's strategy involved capturing pirate ships intact to deny them the ability to regroup and to repurpose the vessels for its own use.

The Royal Navy's success in eradicating piracy was not merely a matter of superior firepower; it was also the result of strategic foresight and coordination. Naval patrols were expanded along key trade routes, ensuring a constant presence that deterred potential attacks. Pirate networks were systematically dismantled through a combination of military action, legal reform, and intelligence gathering.

The navy worked closely with colonial administrations and private interests to identify pirate threats and neutralize them.

By the mid-18th century, the Royal Navy's supremacy had effectively ended the Golden Age of Piracy. Its ability to project power across vast oceans and adapt to the challenges of maritime warfare established Britain as the preeminent naval force of the era. This dominance not only secured trade routes and colonial holdings but also laid the groundwork for the Pax Britannica, a period of relative global peace maintained by British naval hegemony.

***

The Golden Age of Piracy was drawing to a close. Increased naval patrols, international cooperation, and stricter enforcement of anti-piracy laws had made the seas increasingly inhospitable for pirates. Despite these mounting pressures, some pirate crews persisted, clinging to their dangerous way of life. However, their final battles and diminishing returns marked the end of an era, as piracy became less profitable and survivable.

The capture and execution of pirate crews became a common outcome during these final years. Courts of Admiralty were established in key colonial locations, streamlining the prosecution of captured pirates. Trials were often swift, and sentences were harsh, with public hangings used to deter others from turning to piracy. The executions of high-profile pirates reinforced the message that piracy was no longer a viable or sustainable occupation.

As the risks of piracy increased, its rewards diminished. Merchant ships began to travel in well-defended convoys, protected by naval escorts and outfitted with improved weaponry. The profits from successful raids were often outweighed by the dangers of encountering well-armed crews or naval patrols. Additionally, the economic conditions that had fueled piracy, such as unemployment following the end of major wars, began to stabilize, offering former sailors alternative livelihoods.

The diminishing returns of piracy were not only financial but also logistical. The lack of resources and safe havens forced pirate crews to operate in increasingly remote areas, where opportunities for plunder were fewer and farther between. Some pirates attempted to establish new bases of operation in regions like Madagascar or along the West African coast, but these efforts were often short-lived due to isolation, disease, and the absence of reliable support networks.

Piracy did not disappear entirely. Smaller-scale acts of maritime banditry persisted in poorly regulated areas, and isolated groups of pirates continued to operate well into the 18th century. However, these later pirates lacked the resources, organization, and legendary status of their predecessors. By the mid-1700s, piracy had been reduced to a shadow of its former self, confined to the fringes of maritime trade and largely overshadowed by the dominance of colonial navies.

Afterword

Beyond the myths of treasure maps and swashbuckling adventurers lies a more complex reality, one that reflects the social, economic, and political upheavals of the early modern world. This book has sought to explore the many facets of piracy, peeling back the layers of legend to reveal the historical truths beneath. Pirates, often demonized in their own time and romanticized in ours, lived lives shaped by both desperation and audacity, challenging the systems that sought to control them while leaving behind a legacy that continues to fascinate.

Piracy is a mirror reflecting broader human themes. The allure of freedom on the high seas, the rejection of authority, and the creation of self-governed communities resonate far beyond the confines of maritime history. Their stories endure not because they were heroes, but because they embody a fundamental human desire to defy the odds and live on one's own terms. As we have seen, the realities of piracy were far from glamorous. Life aboard a pirate ship was harsh and dangerous, marked by constant threats of disease, injury, and betrayal. The economic pressures and systemic injustices that drove many to piracy were harsh realities of their era.

The seas that once teemed with pirate ships are quieter now, but their echoes remain. In every tale of hidden treasures, every depiction of the Jolly Roger, and every imagined life of adventure, the spirit of piracy lives on. May their stories continue to inspire curiosity, reflection, and a deeper understanding of the complex world they inhabited.

Thank you for your attention to my book!

Arthur Weiss, 2024.

Printed in Great Britain
by Amazon